Amy and Dave's COVID Escape Trip - 2021

Amy and Dave's COVID Escape Trip - 2021

David Stoeckl

Albedo Books

Albedo Books
Sequim, WA
albedobooks@gmail.com

Cover design by Dave Stoeckl
Interior design by Dave Stoeckl

Amy and Dave's COVID Escape Trip - 2021   p.cm.

ISBN: 978-1-967695-16-4 – ebook
        978-1-967695-17-1 – Printed Book

For further information, contact Albedo Books at
albedobooks@gmail.com

This book is written without using any AI

Amy and Dave's COVID Escape Tour – 2021

Hi. I'm Dave. Married to Amy. We live in Sequim, WA, on the Olympic Peninsula. A beautiful place to be sure.

After the COVID crap of 2020 when everyone and their mum had to stay indoors and couldn't venture farther than the grocery store, it was not surprising that many would want to get away from home in 2021. We decided to be part of that group of red-blooded Americans, seeking sanity and an escape from the mundane existences of home life.

With that said, there are always so many things one can do around home. We got some of those home projects done. We painted the outside of the house. I built an extension on our backyard deck, then replaced the existing deck. We installed a 10 X 12 gazebo on the newly replaced deck, adding chairs and plants and more to make it a fine place to congregate for BBQ's or whatever.

We planted a garden for the first time in 2020. I always had a garden when I lived in Birch Bay, WA, up near the Canadian border. We moved to Sequim, eventually bought a house and after other outdoor improvements, took the time and bother of the coronavirus to cultivate and plant lots of yummy items. My corn didn't turn out very well, but my tomatoes loved it, and my jalapenos thrived like never before. As the autumn weather cooled, I moved the plants into the greenhouse. My last harvest of jalapenos was in December, 2020.

So, with all that accomplished, we considered taking a vacation in 2021. COVID had relented a bit. We didn't have to wear face masks in the stores and all that. The Delta variant was not yet big news.

Amy works for the Port Angeles School District, so she has two and a half months of summer off work. We discussed what kind of trip we wanted to take. Europe was on our radar, particularly Portugal and Greece. We'd considered moving to Portugal for a year – may still happen. Also, I'd completed composing a novel called Patmos, about the Apostle John who was exiled and received the prophesies we now call the Book of Revelation. Patmos has been for sale on Amazon Books since February, 2019. I'd composed a few other books after that, but presently was not writing anything, so a trip fit my schedule perfectly.

Had we followed that idea, this would certainly be a very different book. European travel has been mostly open, but that could change at anytime.

Thus, we instead opted to follow one of Amy's dreams. She had always wanted to get a motorhome and travel around the US. Amy herself is not much of a driver, but I'm a drivaholic. I love driving the open road, ever seeking a road I've never driven down before. That became the goal. Could we do it? Could we afford it? Where would we go? All that jazz.

ANTICIPATION

Part of the preparation and planning is as much part of the trip as the actual journey. We chatted about where we'd like to go, but it wasn't until I bought a large US map at Dollar Tree, and placed some Post-It pointer flags that the trip took on its first dimensions of reality. There were no holds. No rules. Wherever we might want to go we placed on that map. This was the Dream Sheet. This was the What If? This was the Maybe or Maybe Not. Anywhere either of us wanted to go, we would flag it.

After a week or two of that map covering our dining table, (a place we seldom eat if the truth be known), we started looking at dates. First, Amy got out of school June 17th. Another cast-in-stone-date was July 25-28 – a Stoeckl Family Reunion near Florence, OR. My nephew Kevin had passed away from colon cancer in 2020. We could not gather for his memorial in 2020, so waited a year. My Aunt Annie also passed away in spring, 2021, so we could honor her as well.

As the map and a calendar came together, it became apparent some of our destinations would have to be cut. Key West was the first to go. Niagara Falls and Boston got chopped. Amy had friends and family in Delaware and Maryland. Sorry. We wouldn't have time to get to the East Coast and back to Oregon by July 25th, along with all the other places we targeted closer west.

I spent lots of hours pouring over possible routes. I printed maps of the US and drew lines from destination to destination, listing dates at the bottom of the page. Everything was still a Maybe. If you're visiting Mount Rushmore, you can show-up any day of the week, but if you're visiting friends and family, it has to coincide with their schedules and itineraries and whatever. Also, some were still scared of COVID, so didn't want anyone coming to their homes.

As the itinerary started to take form, we contacted family and friends and found those who would love for us to grace their homes for a day or two.

The trip would be somewhat circular. I created two possible routes, but we were more inclined to try to make the southern part of the trip first when it was potentially cooler than would be later in the summer.

There was so much we wanted to see. The Grand Canyon. Arches National Park. Mount Rushmore. Arkansas has been the last state of the fifty I've never gotten to visit. Somehow, I'd always gone past it to the north, south, east of west. We would be seeing family in Joplin, MO, plus seeing some shows in Branson, MO, just a few miles from the Arkansas border. We were going to Arkansas.

So, as the route became more and more real, tweaked and established with those we would visit, I finally printed off my last US map to mark the roads and where we'd go. It's so funny to see it printed off before you go, because it's so plain and sanitary as you look at it, but it represents an adventure like no other that can only be experienced once we actually leave.

THE MOTORHOME

We're not rich people. We had some extra money set aside for the trip, but we are regular, working-class folks. We knew we had to have a motor home that could actually make the trip – a tall order when you don't have more than say ten grand to spend on the RV. We checked Craigslist and Facebook Marketplace. We looked at a few motorhomes, but never found the one we thought could make the trip and be big enough as well as comfortable for us.

We looked at a Bounder in Joyce, WA – a well cared for vehicle, and I think that one would have been good, but we were not that ready to buy when we looked at it. We checked some others locally, but living out on the Olympic Peninsula, one becomes accustomed to having to drive farther to get what one wants. That goes for medical schtuff, various stores, restaurants, shows, sporting events, etc. Seattle is over two hours away. Seatac Airport a tad closer. Sometimes we would take one of the four ferries, though to be honest, when going to Seatac or Seattle, we usually drove south through the Tacoma Narrows and paid the six bucks toll, rather than twenty bucks for a ferry each way.

The one exception was Mariner games. It is perfect to take the Bainbridge Island Ferry to downtown Seattle, walking on. Much cheaper than taking my car. It is like only a 15-20 minute walk to the stadium. We enjoyed that ferry for other shows we caught in the big city, or to take visiting friends to Pikes Place Market and other Seattle sites. The ferry becomes part of the fun.

One big consideration was that our home has a back driveway off the alleyway that's made for an RV –

whether trailer or motorhome. It measures thirty feet from the house to the gate, but with the eave, I might have been able to fit a flat faced motorhome of 27 or 28 feet in length overall. Not a bad size for a motorhome.

So, what did we get? Did we stay within the size limit? Nope. When we found our baby, we knew it was the right one. A 1990 Tiffin Allegro, 31' long. It had a bathroom and shower along with a separate bedroom in the back. No slide outs. Amy didn't want any slide outs because she was concerned they would be the first thing to break down.

The best feature on this rig was the engine and tranny. It had the 5.2 liter Cummins diesel engine and an Allison tranny. From my work with Dodge many years back, plus working for Blaine Public Works up on the US/Canada border, I knew both that engine and tranny to be very reliable.

We found this Allegro in Olympia – 100 miles away from Sequim. We arranged to see two motor homes while there. The first one was a NO pretty much from the start, but when we saw the Allegro, though older, it seemed more like home. You know how it is. Some vehicles just touch you as better when you drive them. Even though this one was 31 years old, the diesel engine had 93,000 miles – barely broke in for this diesel. This is the same engine you'll find in a Bluebird School Bus. When I worked for Dodge in Salt Lake City, a school district employee told me they retired the school buses after half a million miles. 93,000 miles ain't anywhere close.

The brakes were mushy. The seller, named Maurice, said he would have the brakes bled and we'd be back in a few days to get it. True to his word, the brakes were far, far better when we returned. With that said, we were still foolish buyers. The blinkers didn't work right. The cruise control didn't work. The dash fan didn't work. Other items, but the price allowed us to put a bit more into the vehicle before our adventure would begin. Maurice asked $8,500, accepted my offer for 8 grand, and we became proud owners of a 31 year old motor home that had been at the top of its class when built.

Driving home, it kept threatening to overheat, the needle in the red zone. I stopped along the winding two lane road following Hood Canal, with Amy following, and checked the engine. Nothing smelled hot, so I continued and got it home with no mishaps. We determined later that some of the electrical wiring under the dash caused the instrument panel to not read correctly - another one of the repairs we had done before departing.

We had this beautiful driveway in the back, but still had to park it in the front driveway. It's there right now as I write. It's always funny how quickly one becomes accepting of such a change in our regular lives. I had to trim back some tree branches, but otherwise it fit perfectly.

We took the RV to Eric's RV Repair in Sequim. Eric's a very friendly and likeable person, but I wouldn't recommend taking your vehicle to him. They claimed they fixed the dash fan. It wasn't fixed, so they charged me another $110 to fix it again. And, even then it still didn't work right once we left. The fuel gauge worked fine the first time I took it in, then didn't work when I got it home. When I took it in the second time, they charged me another $110 to tell me it wasn't working and maybe I should put a couple bottles of Seafoam in the fuel – maybe that would loosen up the float so the gauge would work again. That's what I did, and it did work, but should not have cost me $110 for that info. For another $110, they allegedly checked the cruise control for an entire hour, and reported to me that it would need to be replaced. That's $330 of nothing I was charged for the second visit.

Either way, we got the blinker fixed. Being diesel, it has a 30-gallon propane tank for the stove and generator. The generator showed only 84 hours total use in 31 years – not much use at all, and it worked like a charm each time we had to use it. Eric's made sure there were no leaks in the propane lines. We did get some value from Eric's but not a thousand dollars worth, so I shan't be taking our Allegro back whenever it needs more work.

We also had the oil changed and tranny oil changed elsewhere.

There were two headlights out which I replaced. The bright lights were also needing the connections cleaned. The antifreeze reservoir was cracked, so I replaced that. A couple other lights needed replacing, but for the most part, it was more than ready to go. I got a new battery for the engine. It had a dual battery set up for the interior lights which seemed okay at the time.

We got the Allegro like six-seven weeks before departure, so plenty to do before we would leave. What's even crazier, because of the lengthy time Eric's had the RV, we never had a chance to try it out camping before we left. Not even one night.

Another problem is that I'm around six and a half feet tall. I don't know if you've ever tried RV beds, but they're classically shorter than a normal bed. This one was cloth wrapped around foam rubber – probably the original bed with two corners lopped off for easier access to the sides of the bedroom. We knew before we bought it that we would need a larger bed. So, I found a full queen-sized mattress online for fifty bucks that would be perfect. I paid more than that for the plywood to extend the platform, securing the wood to the box that contained the fresh water tank and we had a good bed that was plenty long enough for me.

One thing we considered was whether to tow my car behind. I asked Eric what kind of fuel mileage I should get with the Allegro, and he estimated around Ten MPG. I then asked what mileage I'd get if I towed my car and he answered, "Around ten MPG."

I have a Solara Convertible, so driving with the top down is very attractive for me. I think Amy gets tired of it at times. I never do. We looked at getting a tow dolly. Prices were around a grand for the mini-trailer. The more we discussed it, the more we decided to not tow a car with us.

Instead, we bought a $50 bike rack that fit into the tow hitch. I brought my bicycle and Amy brought her little battery powered scooter. They were not ideal since the scooter only goes a few miles on a full charge, and it was not like I wanted to ride the bike any farther than that as well, but we brought both and used them sparingly on the trip.

Other considerations? It would have been a bit cheaper to drive my Solara the whole way and lodge at motels. The gas mileage vs. the Allegro would have been more than enough to pay for lodging, but we'd also eat out more, digging deeply into any savings. The motorhome became that much more attractive. When we stayed with someone, we could still 'sleep in our own bed'. That's all part of the attraction of an RV.

HIGH SCHOOL GRADUATE

We had a child graduating from high school in 2021. They still weren't doing the graduating ceremonies, so we bought cap and gown, took our own pics, and sent out announcements. The graduation would be held just over a week before our departure date of June 18th.

Amy's mom, who lives in the tiny town of Julesburg, CO, came to attended the graduation. Her health isn't very good, so having the get together at our home instead of a big ordeal at the school, was plenty for her.

But the big question became how to get her back to the airport before we left? As the plans came together, she would be flying out the morning we wanted to depart. We had to do a practice run the day before we left, to make sure she could get into the motorhome. She struggled and was slow, of course, but I'm pleased to say she was able to get in and out. If she'd not been able to climb into the motorhome, I offered to drive her in my car to Seatac, drop her off, drive back home, then leave on our trip – another five hours of driving before we even left. Fortunately, she was able to be taken to the airport in our Allegro. Yay!

13

ARTANIS

Another consideration was one of our dogs, a nine-pound little mongrel named Artanis. He sleeps with us, and Amy is his favorite person on earth. We talked about taking him with us throughout all plans, but as we came closer to leaving and wondering how he would do if left in the motorhome by himself, we started thinking maybe it'd be better to not bring along the dog.

We have three dogs. Two of the kids, ages 23 and 18, have been home. The younger one I mentioned just graduated from high school. The other is in his last year of college. When COVID hit in February of 2020, he was attending the University of Alaska in Fairbanks. All the classes became online classes, so he came home, partially to save money and partially because he was living in a dry cabin – no running water or sewer. He had a dog named Mira, short for Miracle, who fit right in with our canines. We also had a mini-Aussie named Esme who belongs to the 18 year old, and an old cat named Cooper.

So, almost last minute, we talked with the son about taking care of Artanis. Artanis actually had been his high school graduation present in 2018, but this dog definitely did not have enough hair to survive Alaskan winters. So, he became Amy's dog while her son was off to college far, far away. Poor Artanis was confused at first, especially when our son would come home for a visit, but eventually time with us, sleeping under the covers at the foot of our bed, we became his preferred norm. Leaving him for a month and a half would have him wondering what gives, but it was still the better option, and many times during our adventure, we

14

realized what we would not have been able to do if we'd had our precious, little doggie with us.

PURPOSE OF THIS BOOK

I guess it would be nice to add a little paragraph, like an Introduction or Forward, to say as I considered this book, I thought of two main points to focus on. One is RV life – always a welcome consideration for people who live in RV's, trailers, camper vans, etc. The second it to share the areas we visited. Some will be friends and family, but with the PURPOSE OF THIS BOOK in mind, I'll try to also share the fun and interesting parts of the region. With that said, lets dive into the trip.

SEQUIM, WASHINGTON AND
THE OLYMPIC PENINSULA

When someone does travel writing, they often wait until they're gone on some wild adventure to take pics and write about what they've seen and done. I've not done a bunch of travel writing, but I do know I could write volumes about where I live. The Olympic Peninsula has books of its own already composed, telling of this remarkable chunk of real estate.

First, the Olympic Peninsula could be identified with its five counties: Clallam, Jefferson, Kitsap, Mason and Grays Harbor. The Olympic National Park and the accompanying Olympic National Forest takes up roughly half of the peninsula. Parts of the park are part of all five counties. Along the north side of the peninsula are three main cities – Port Angeles, Sequim and Port Townsend, (32 miles east of Sequim). The locals call Port Angeles PA and Port Townsend PT.

Sequim is pronounced like "Squim," not like the word sequin.

Forks might be the fourth city, way out toward the west end of the peninsula. That's where the Twilight movies were filmed, so have some vampire signs posted around the city, and a duplicate of Bella's truck by the Visitor Center.

I can see the mountains from my home office, although looking at a map, I think it's not actually the National Park, but a section called the Buckhorn Wilderness. It's all treated in some ways as the National Park. The houses of Sequim head as far south as the road takes them, then gets shut off by the range of mountains.

Sequim itself is the second largest city in Clallam County, about fifteen miles from Port Angeles, the county seat. It has a population of around 6,600 people. The north side of the city juts up against the Strait of Juan de Fuca.

US Highway 101 used to run right through town, but new construction twenty years back ran the highway along the south side of town with three exits. It's fun to see the signs on the on-ramps that all say, "Highway Entrance" instead of, "Freeway Entrance." Only place I've seen that so far.

Sequim is kind of funny commercially. It's smaller than Port Angeles but has many more box stores including Home Depot and Costco. Situated between Port Angeles and Port Townsend, the stores thought better to build in Sequim to attract PT residents. Their marketing departments were right, so get a fair amount of business from PT who likes being old world quaint and won't allow any large conglomerate businesses within their borders. I understand it took a whole bunch of pressure on McDonald's part to get Port Townsend to agree to having the restaurant.

There's an awesome bike trail called the Olympic Discovery Trail, that stretches from Port Townsend to the Pacific coast, (or vice versa). Lots of picture opportunities along the way, from mountains to ocean to rivers and lakes.

Sequim has mostly retired folks living here – over 50% of the population. The locals have been known to say that "Port Angeles is full of old people, and their parents live in Sequim." Plenty of accommodations for the aged but makes it hard to get bonds passed for the school district.

The best places to eat in Sequim? We like Oak Table, a breakfast and lunch restaurant. Slightly fancy and really good food. 101 Diner has the 50's motif. There's a Black Bear Diner near the Holiday Inn Express on the east side of town. Sergio's has the best Mexican food, though a lot of people also like Baja Cantina. Bentos offers large portions for teriyaki and rice.

Sequim allegedly is located in a rain shadow, so gets less rain than Port Angeles. It has the nickname The Big Blue Hole. I worked in Port Townsend for two years, and found PT oftentimes had less rain than Sequim. I jokingly have the theory that the PT folks knew their town was better weatherwise than most of the Pacific Northwest, but they didn't want others to know, so they made up the story that Sequim was the Big Blue Hole so retirees would move there instead.

I've been living in Sequim since 2016, and have been blessed to become part of this community. During the summer, they have free concerts on stage at Carrie

Blake Park. They have a log show every year, plus the Lavender Festival and the Irrigation Festival – the latter being the oldest annual festival in Washington State. With all the retirees, they have pickleball courts, right next to the skate park. Lots of elk in the surrounding wilderness and mountains.

Amy and I are pleased to attend the Carlsborg Family Church in the little town of Carlsborg, directly west of Sequim. I lead the worship team, playing guitar, and Amy sings.

On the Strait of Juan de Fuca is the Dungeness Bay and Dungeness Spit. At the end of the five-mile-long spit is a lighthouse. If you want to hike to the lighthouse, you have to watch the tide tables and begin your trek when the tide is waning. It's obnoxious to walk the spit when the tide is high.

Overall, a lovely little town. I can see the Olympic Mountains from my office window and back yard. Living in town, almost everything is close enough to walk to if I wanted.

THURSDAY, JUNE 17th

It's funny. No matter how much you plan and write down what to bring and so on, there are still so many things to do last minute as I prepared the Allegro for the trip. I won't bore you with such mundane details, but I was running non-stop all day packing the motor home. I totally expected to be done by early afternoon, but as 9:00 and 10:00 pm arrived, we were still working on getting everything ready...

FRIDAY, JUNE 18TH
SEATAC AIRPORT IN A MOTORHOME?

The plan was to leave early Friday morning, June 18th. Amy's last day of work for the PA School District was the 17th, so she was gone much of the day, then joined me mid-afternoon getting everything ready. Her mom's flight was around 10 a.m. the next morning, so we'd have to leave by 6 a.m. to get her to Seatac on time. She would need a wheelchair when she arrived. She was sure she was not going to make her flight, even when the airline staff were taking her in the wheelchair.

There's a grand feeling when the planned trip actually begins. Don't you LOVE that feeling? We had it in smaller measure as we backed out of the driveway and headed on our way. Amy took some pics of the Allegro leaving before climbing aboard.

We'd just left town, on Highway 101, when Amy asked if I had grabbed her mom's suitcase. Nope. Neither had she, so we had to turn around and put ourselves around twenty minutes later driving back to the house, get the suitcase and begin again our journey.

The two plus hours to Seatac actually went without as much traffic slowing us down as I feared. Reaching the Tacoma Narrows toll booths, I stayed on the freeway. The state sends you a toll charge through the mail. It's a buck more, but would be worth it to save the minute or two getting to Seatac. Oddly, now a few months since that day, I never received the $7.00 charge in the mail. Or it got tossed as junk mail by the kids or something. I keep awaiting a higher charge for non-payment, but it's never shown up, either.

Maneuvering a 31' motorhome at Seatac Departures makes for fun driving. It wasn't the busiest I've seen, but still lots of cars. I just went ahead and parked in bus parking. No bus came and it turned out just fine. Amy's mum said bye, Amy made sure she got her wheelchair and attendant, then we could safely head out on the open road.

Dave at SeaTac Airport with Morris in Loading Zone

Leaving Seatac and swooping up I-405 to head around the east of side of Lake Washington and Seattle, we felt the pull of the road. That was for each of us the real start of our COVID Escape Tour.

Along I-90 eastbound, you leave the city and congestion for the Cascade Range. The highest point is Snoqualmie Pass, heading up to 2,726 feet above sea level. This was the first real test for our old motorhome, and he did just fine.

When a person buys an older used vehicle, there's always in your mind the possibility that all our plans and mapping and scheduling with friends and family can immediately get thrown out the window with a breakdown. We were somewhat cavalier in our discussions along those lines. What if we broke down near Tucumcari, NM and were stuck there for a week or two? So be it. That's where we'd spend our vacation time. Actually, it'd be somewhat sad to lose all the money. We'd prepaid for most of the RV sites, plus show tickets in Branson, MO. We couldn't be sure what we'd be able to get refunded.

I-90 is a beautiful stretch of road as you leave the Seattle metropolitan area, and pass by heavy laden forests of evergreen trees, clinging to the side of the mountains like a crewcut.

Leaving town so early, we had not taken time to eat. North Bend would be the next town of size as we drove through the mountains. We maneuvered through the narrow streets and found a perfect place to parallel park near the Twede's Cafe. With some COVID restrictions still in place, their seating was wider apart than before the _plandemic_, so took a short wait to get a seat. They gave us a hockey puck that lit up and sang a song for us

22

when our seats were ready. The time gave us a chance to walk through town, stretch legs and see a few of the sites.

North Bend is a little smaller than Sequim. No big stores at all. It's in the Snoqualmie Valley, still part of King County which is Seattle's county. There's a beautiful little mountain called Mount Si directly to the north, poking up like God's pinky off the valley floor.

Twede's Café was basic breakfast fare, not overpriced and I would totally recommend it. The food came quickly enough, and we enjoyed our little visit.

As I said earlier, we didn't have a working fuel gauge, so I considered refueling every two hundred miles or so. We filled up at the Shell station and continued on our way.

DESTINATION ELLENSBURG

After you top the long climb to Snoqualmie Pass, the road levels out a bunch and doesn't try to take you down the other side like a bunch of mountain passes. A few miles past the summit, you pass beautiful Lake Keechelus. You have to plan ahead and exit I-90 at Snoqualmie Pass to visit the lake picnic area. Staying on I-90, there's virtually nowhere to stop along the way.

At this point, I-90 basically heads straight southeast towards Ellensburg, less than an hour down the road. The way is still mostly mountains and trees, then with virtually no fanfare or official announcement, you're leaving the trees for flat, barren areas, treeless rolling hills and basically a close to desert climate. The change is truly remarkable.

Ellensburg, population 21,000 plus, is the centerpiece for Kittitas County. It's also the junction for I-90 and I-82. My son Paul lives there.

Paul's a Young Adults Pastor for the Mercer Creek Church. He's been there around ten years. His close friend Jo Jo Hahn, who he grew up with in Utah, is the Worship Leader.

Paul is married to Alicia. They have two wonderful children, Liam and Finley. Now, it's always, always, always a thrill for grandpa to see his grandkids. The distance is such that we don't get to see them often enough. They loved that Grandpa and Grandma came in a motorhome. Liam thought that was our only home.

Of course, they wanted to play in the motorhome as much as they could. I have to say here, Amy is amazing. I love seeing the kids, but I don't plan or bring schtuff for them to do. Amy does. She works as a Speech Language Pathologist at an elementary school. She knows all about how to entertain the youngsters, and filled two drawers in our RV with games and toys. Liam and Finley always love when we come see them.

Finley decided to call Amy "Nanny." We don't know why. When her mom, Alicia, questioned her daughter, Finley just said she was Nanny.

They also thought the RV was our only home. That we lived in it full time. Smiley face.

They played hide and seek in the RV, always hiding in the same places. The doorway has a platform that covers the stairs. We never use it, but it created a fun place for the kids to hide, on the stairs, under the platform with the door open.

Amy also got some little cars that were gyros, and spun around on your finger or the table or atop the provided cones.

Paul is the main cook for his household. I expect Alicia knows how to cook just fine, but I don't recall ever having anything she prepared.

I told Amy before we even left, I expected Mexican food would be offered everywhere we stayed. I wasn't quite accurate, but it did become a personal joke between us. Paul made tacos for dinner, but don't think to compare these with Taco Bell, or even the tacos your mum made. He diced up some fancy peppers to add to the meat. He crushed cilantro and such to place on your tacos, plus more ingredients that I don't exactly remember. Very fancy. I don't make them that fancy at my house, to be sure. It was quite the treat.

We could only stay one day. Before we left, we took Paul and the kids for a little ride around the neighborhood in the Allegro. Memorable thrill for them to be sure.

SATURDAY, JUNE 19th

As I mentioned, Amy and I were new to traveling and living by motorhome, so our next destination could not have been more perfect. In the tiny town of Fruitland, WA lives my brother Jay and his wife Jennifer. They breed Dire Wolf Project dogs. Jennifer has written a book on her breeding. They are a beautiful and remarkable breed, much sought after.

J&J have lived on a twenty-eight acres spread over the last four years. More remarkably for our trip, they've been living in the motorhome they bought before they even purchased the land. Living in a motorhome for four years has certainly taught them a few lessons about RV living, and they were both pleased to share their experiences with us, plus check out our RV, give us their assessment, etc.

The most amusing thing you see when you arrive is that they live in old motorhome, but their dogs have well made kennels to dwell in, sturdy and made to provide adequate warmth and protection from the very cold, snowy winters.

They also had a puppy who lived inside with them. Its mother lost her milk, so they had to nurture the dog. Its rear legs had not developed properly from lack of nutrition, so they were trying to get him to back to full strength for his age. He was very timid. He loved playing with you on the couch, but when you got up, he wouldn't dare jump off. His legs were not yet strong enough.

Jay is ten years younger than me. He has a twin brother named John who lives in Grants Pass, OR – whom we visited later this trip.

One of the first things Jay did, besides guide us to a fairly flat place to park, was bring out a solar panel. They have two hooked to their RV 24/7. He had a third he wasn't using, so we hooked it to our interior lights' batteries. Even better, when we left, Jay lent us the solar panels to use for the rest of our trip. We would be getting together in late July for the family reunion and could return it, then.

If you boondock at all, (ie, stay in remote areas), solar panels are a true godsend. There's a bunch of power from the sun virtually every day, to help recharge the batteries.

Actually, Jay tested the coach batteries and found them to be lacking. We were playing a game in our RV one evening and the lights started dimming way too early. The next day, Jay took us to Costco in Spokane, a seventy-mile drive, to get batteries for around half the price we would have paid locally. I would have liked to support the local business and all that, but paying over $300 for a couple batteries was not the best use of my financial resources. The trip to Spokane also turned into part of the adventure. Jay and Jenn took us to D. Lish's Hamburgers – one of his favorite fast-food eateries. I give it two thumbs-up as well.

One thing I often do before working on a vehicle is take pictures of what I'm working on before I start. I did the same with the batteries so we would not have to totally rely on our memories, first when buying the new batteries, and second, when hooking them up again. We'd removed the two 12-volt batteries to bring them with us for core trade-in.

The big consideration was whether to get two 6 Volt batteries, or two 12 Volt Batteries. You hook them

27

together differently for your RV, but still they supply 12 Volts to the system. If I'd hooked up the two 12 Volt batteries like the 6 Volt, I'd be sending 24 Volts to the system and screw up the electrical wiring. Probably burst any light bulbs when turned on. You get the idea.

At Costco we discussed the pros and cons of the 6 or 12 Volt systems. The 6 Volt batteries are considered the better system, but we decided it would be best to stay with what was already set up, and changed out the 12 Volt batteries. The 6 Volt were also taller. I was pretty sure I had clearance, but when you're 70 miles away from your rig, you're less inclined to take uneducated chances.

Jay also showed me how to use the awning. We had not tried to bring it out before departure. Unfortunately, we were parked too close to a tree for the awning to go out full sail, and the screen door scraped a hole in the awning. Still, it was good to try it out, see how it worked, and know what to do the next time we wanted to bring it out.

The awning would have been used more, but the main places we stayed for more than a day – Topeka, KS, Lincoln, NB, and Julesburg, CO, are all part of the tornado zones. Big, windy storms at any time, so I kept the awning in when I otherwise might have used it.

Jay also tested the batteries for Amy's scooter and found one of the four not holding a charge. We replaced that one as well. (I probably should mention that we bought a bike stand that in mounted via the tow hitch. We brought both a bicycle for myself and an electric scooter for Amy. Without towing a car, these could prove very useful for our quick trips.

In short, Jay loved our RV. He stated it was top of its class when it was constructed. The wood interior. The TV's and such. The engine and tranny. Just a well-made motorhome.

THE EMERSONS

After we'd been there a couple days, one of their closest friends came to visit, named Joe Emerson. We shared food and beer and so forth. Joe played guitar very well, mostly leads, so all of us were able to jam together for a couple hours. Just had a delightful time.

Then on Sunday, we attended church services with Jay and Jenn and met an elderly couple, Don and Selena Emerson, and their daughter Rose. Joe's family. Delightful people to get to know as well, if only for a few minutes at the church.

Somewhere in the mix, we were given a very small book that told the story of the Emerson's. Their son Donnie, who we were not able to meet, lives in Spokane. Joe's younger brother. They had two other siblings as well, but they never came up in conversation.

Amy and I started reading the Emerson's short biography. I'll give you the even quicker version.

Donald Emerson owned seventeen-hundred acres. They did logging, farming and ranching for a bit of livestock. They had no radio or record players, etc. in their home in the late 1970's, but Donald bought a tractor which did have a radio. Teenaged Donnie would listen to the radio while working the farm. He started to show a very natural talent for music, learning first guitar, but expanding to any instrument he could get his hands on. As Donnie started composing music, Joe learned to play drums.

The next thing that occurred amazes me, even as I tell you. Daddy Donald was so impressed with his son's talent for music, he took a second mortgage on the land and built a recording studio on the property. I got to see the outside of the studio – just a plain wooden building, about 12' by 20'. Not real big, but surely adequate.

Donald spent quite a lot on the recording equipment, musical instruments and even a top-of-the-line Moog synthesizer. After Donnie completed his chores for the day, he'd spend his evenings in the studio, learning the ins and outs of music recording. He and Joe, aged 15 and 17, recorded like nine songs, pressed into vinyl records. The album, called Dreamin' Wild you can hear on Spotify.

Of course, the album didn't sell at all. No promotion. No distribution, etc.

They put out two more albums which did no better than the first.

Dad then mortgaged the farm further to build a performing venue, simply called The Barn. Again, it's fifty miles from any town of size, in the middle of the property. They had ceased raising cattle, so didn't need the barn anymore. There is a stage and seating for about 300 people, but even more impressive, across the barn from the stage is an upper-level walkway. Daddy Donald designed it to be able to lay down the wall of the barn to become a second performing venue. When I toured the barn, I noticed the many electrical outlet on that wall, and Rose told us the wall could be laid down to become another stage. Very inventive!

Nowadays, it's used for weddings and other rented family celebrations.

Well, with so much of the farm mortgaged for Donnie to make a name as a musical performer, the bank wound up taking fifteen-hundred of their acres. The family now has only two-hundred acres where Joe and Donald ,Sr. still do their logging business. Yet, when we spoke with Donald, he has absolutely no regrets at what they did to help Donnie.

Donnie still works fulltime composing and performing music in Spokane, writing jingles and such.

Now I didn't know this, but there are people who call themselves "Lo-Fi", who search for golden gems of music that never made it. I may be sketchie with the details, but as I learned, in 2017 one of these Lo-Fi folks found Donnie and Joe's record, Dreamin' Wild, in a pawn shop, and fell in love with it. He contacted Donnie, now in his fifties, and said he wanted to re-release it under a different record label. The record has in fact been re-released.

It's most popular song, called Baby, has now appeared in a couple movies. I don't know which movies. Their other music has also been brought up to the 21st century. Still, it's been strange for Donnie and Joe who made this when they were teens. Suddenly, they are being asked to come play these forty-something year old songs. And Joe hasn't really touched a drum set in years.

Even more remarkable, at the time we visited them, Universal Pictures was preparing to make a movie about their lives. Joe said they looked over the manuscript and it had a bunch of crap that never happened, conflicts between parents and kids, etc. Both

Donnie and Joe objected to the script. If they couldn't take their mum to the movie, it wasn't acceptable. I recently learned that a script was approved and filming has begun.

As I said, Daddy Donald said he never rued any decisions to help his sons, but now that it's being considered for a major motion picture, he wouldn't mind getting some of that cash back.

Amy grew up on a wheat farm in Colorado and Nebraska. When I read to her the account and they lost the farm, etc., she was literally in tears. She knew the sacrifices farmers made. That made Daddy Donald's decision to build the recording studio all the more amazing for her.

Before we left, we were able to visit The Barn. Rose was cleaning it up for a wedding. We took some typical, nice group pics of us and The Barn. Then we went next door to the Emerson home. Mother Selena was there, and we got to learn her story.

She was born in Malta. During World War II, her family moved out of their home to hide in caves to avoid German bombings. Their father would head back into town regularly to get provisions for his family.

Selena, a teen during this time, never learned to read and write. To this day, she still doesn't know how to read or write, we are told, but she sure knows how to talk. She'll talk your ears off and still keep going.

Their home is filled to overflowing with pictures of the family. More than most homes I've visited. After we left, we went to Walgreens and printed off the pictures we all took together, enclosed them in a card she couldn't read, and mailed them to her. Rose called us just last week to thank us for the pics.

As a last observation, Joe built a very beautiful home a quarter mile from his birth home, still on family land and right by the recording studio. He's never married, and intentionally never finished the master bedroom because in his words, his bride should have input on how to finish their bedroom. At sixty-two, he doesn't seem all that intent on finding the one woman to complete his life.

Also on his property, he's built a small, but very beautiful chapel. The Emerson family are deeply spiritual in their love for Jesus and their Catholic faith. Amy and I both feared that Universal Pictures would smudge their dynamic faith to water down the story. That would be our one recommendation to them. Don't let them ignore the depths of their Christian faith that has upheld and blessed their family all these years.

MORE ON JAY AND JENN

I cannot fully express how fine a time we had visiting my brother and sister-in-law. We've not been that close over the years, so you never know how the visit is going to go. As our time to depart drew near, we didn't want to leave, and of all the places we visited on our adventure, this one had nothing even remotely negative. It would cost around $300 in diesel fuel to visit them again, round trip, so cannot come back as often as we'd like. We hope to be able to before the winter cold hits, and if not, we'll await next spring.

They bought too much food, as often happens. They have very little space in their RV fridge for leftovers, so we got to take lots of goodies with us. (Our

RV fridge works okay, but can be less than adequate while driving long distances.)

J&J took us for a tour of their property. They're right next to a state park, so no one is going to move in on that side. They have a beautiful view of the Columbia River. The property next door is way overpriced, so they may not have any neighbors to the other side as well anytime soon. If the price came closer to what Jay and Jenn paid for their twenty-eight acres, Jay said they would be tempted to buy it.

They want to build a house. They've been preparing to have the well drilled. That will determine where the house will be, though they also had just had a chunk of land cleared and leveled for their house. They don't want to go into debt, so everything will be built on a cash only pace. They want to continue to live off the grid with their doggies.

I teased them when I first arrived, admitting I didn't know what to expect. Would they be dressed in camo and have confederate flags all over? Nah, but it was fun to imagine.

We ate good food and played lots of music and games in the evening. Just a blessed and wonderful visit. I used to compose a bunch of music. I still write a song here and there – two songs over the last year. Jay requested I play two of my songs from long ago - *An Island*, and *Libby Song (Light the Fire),* both which he recorded as I played them on their deck.

Sidenote: *An Island* I wrote in 1976 in Oahu back when I was stationed at Pearl Harbor. Navy days. I was with friends. We stopped along one of the many beaches one evening, in this case Makaha Beach on the southwestern arm of Oahu. They'd brought their swim trunks, still wet in the trunk of the car. I had not been swimming with them the previous day, but I always took my guitar EVERYWHERE, so though I could not swim with my friends, I was blessed to be able to take a melody I'd composed in Vallejo, CA when I was stationed at Mare Island Naval Shipyard. I'd intended to write it for a good friend of mine named Robin Pederson, but the lyrics wouldn't gel. Thus, sitting there on the beach that evening, I got the idea for *An Island*, and it turned into one of my best songs to date.

Then last year in 2020, Amy, seventeen-year-old Quinnlyn and I were able to fly over to Oahu for Thanksgiving. Amy's sister Carrie and her husband Nate are both Air Force officers, so make a better than usual income. Their home is nothing fancy, but has an awesome, stone swimming pool with hot tub and waterwall.

We had a delightful eleven days there, but one that was very special to me was being able to return to Makaha Beach where I could play *An Island* for everyone.

***Libby Song, (Light the Fire)*,** I wrote in 1975 when stationed in Groton, CT. I had a friend named Daryl, living near Brockton, MA. I went to visit him – what turned into an every-other-week visit during my Navy schooling in Connecticut. He introduced me to the Libby family who lived in Weymouth Landing, MA. They had two daughters, Leanne, and Janice. Leanne was engaged to a young man attending BYU in Provo, UT. Janice and I became somewhat interested in each other, but the distance kept us from it becoming anything more serious.

At the time, I was on fire writing songs. I composed a song for Janice, called *Rainy Day Person*. I met their good friend Siobhan Lorraine. I loved her name, so wrote *Lady Siobhan Lorraine*. Then, in a way just to even out making a song for other members of the family, I wrote *Libby Song*. I love the other two songs, but of all the songs I've composed, Libby Song has become my most commonly played and performed of my compositions.

Back at Jay and Jenn's, I was quite surprised when he requested the song and wanted to record it. My voice needed to be warmed up to reach some of the high notes in *An Island*. I probably should warm up my voice again and re-record a better version for Jay. Or not. Shrug.

TUESDAY, JUNE 22nd
Destination: Hamilton, MT

Leaving Jay and Jenn's, we explored back roads and highways, working our way to I-90 and onto Missoula, then South on Montana Highway 93 to Hamilton, MT to see Amy's friends Jocelyn and Rick.

I have to share that we arrived in Hamilton much later in the day than expected. Instead of departing first thing in the morning, Jay and Jenn took us to see the Emerson's properties. Despite our late departure, I didn't zip straight south to Davenport and I-90, but took Highway 43, crossing east through the Spokane Reservation. Then, we headed south on Highway 231 to meet Highway 2 at Reardan, WA. Highway 2 is a sweet, little highway that's not too cluttered, and takes you past the Spokane Airport to meet I-90.

Spokane slowed us down, being around rush hour combined with road maintenance. We eventually made it to Idaho and stopped at the rest stop before Coeur d'Alene. It's always funny when you're traveling in a motor home for the first time. It feels so big. Stopping at the rest stop, I took a pic of our Allegro next to a box semi. Comparatively, the RV looked so much smaller than I'd expected.

Two other things made us much later than planned. First, as we prepared for the trip, she told me those few times that Jocelyn and Rick lived near Missoula, but she couldn't remember the name of the town. No biggie, and I just planned the excursion to head to Missoula. Now that we were on the road, I asked for the address and learned that they lived in Hamilton, forty-seven miles south of Missoula, ie, about an hour.

The next thing I should have anticipated, but totally spaced on, was that we were entering the Mountain Time Zone. Duh! We lost an hour. So, when added all up, we reached Jocelyn and Rick's after 9 p.m. Fortunately, we could let them know where we were along the way and have a laugh about it when we arrived.

And, what did Jocelyn make for dinner for our arrival? Enchiladas. The Mexican theme continued.

Rick was in the US Navy the same time as Amy's first husband. They were both stationed in Iceland where they met. Both Amy and Jocelyn were pregnant at the time, so became close friends. Amy has that special gift of being in people's lives long, long after the convenience of locality has passed. When we planned our trip, Jocelyn and Rick were a stop readily added though she'd not seen them for like twenty years.

Both were older, as expected, like us, yet they both were thrilled to have us stay. They have a nice middle-class home in the middle of Hamilton. Our motorhome had a few squeeze moments between badly parked vehicles along their street which is paved, but no curb or gutter.

Their back yard was completely fenced with a barbecue which served us our second night. The fire pit helped smoke away some of the mosquitos. Drinks were served while Amy and Jocelyn caught up on those separated years as well as sharing stories alongside Rick from their Iceland days. I got to do a bunch of listening that visit.

Their daughter, Cat (Caitlin), still lives with them. She was the baby Jocelyn carried in Iceland, now all grown up with a two-year old of her own named Laini. Amy, the consummate elementary school worker, shared much time with Laini. Jocelyn thought her granddaughter might me on the spectrum. Nope. Amy the pro recognized no autistic behaviors.

Life in Montana has surprisingly rural attitudes, totally appropriate in this small city. Rick was a retired Chief Petty Officer and policeman. He loved hunting – a love that was passed on to Cat. Even with baby Laini, she would still go deer hunting when the season allowed, bringing her young 'un with her. No reason to give-up deer hunting just 'cuz you had a baby. You still gotta eat. It is an intriguing attitude for life.

We were able to park out front of their property. No curb and gutter – just a wide swath of dirt covering each side of the road. Level enough I didn't have to place boards under the tires. Rick brought out an extension cord to reach across the front lawn. Amy and Jocelyn sometimes enjoyed visiting in the RV more than the house, back yard or wherever. Also, they had a toddler swing set up off a tree branch in the front yard. Laini was in Seventh-Heaven.

I had considered replacing the passenger wiper on the RV before we left, but since I'd driven it so little and not much rain when I did drive it, it was easily overlooked. For whatever reason we do what we do, in Hamilton Rick and I took to task to replace the blade.

Usually, that's an easy task to perform. I've replaced wipers on my cars and trucks plenty of times, but my Allegro had a different type of wiper than any I'd yet encountered. Not that it was weird. It wasn't. In fact it was so plain, it would be easily ignored. The body is very thin – half the width of most regular wipers today. It was only twenty-one inches long, held on with a single lock nut. The wiper would be positioned parallel with the wiper arm, or turned to whatever position I might have preferred.

The end of the wiper went off the window to the right side when in motion. I tried turning it, which was fine, but it bugged me to have the two wipers not in similar line. Looked like something was wrong when it was actually right.

Rick and I removed the wiper to bring along. Rick took me to AutoZone. Nope. They spent in inordinate amount of time trying to find a solution, but when all was said and done, we could not find a wiper that could be mounted to the wiper arm. Very sad.

I re-bent the arm and cleaned the rubbery blade and all trying to get it to wipe cleaner. It sometimes helped a little, but typically left an unwiped windshield with smeared, dirty water across passenger vision. Not good. Bending the arm helped a bit, but never did get a clean swipe. Since AutoZone could not help, we left town with the same sucky wiper. Our one blessing in all was that it was summertime. Not much rain or snow in the forecast.

Barbecued elk for dinner, from their personal hunted stock. It'd been a long time since I'd had elk, so a treat to get reacquainted. More time around the backyard fire, guitar music and never-ending conversations on life now and then.

THURSDAY, JUNE 24th

We enjoyed coffee in the RV with Jocelyn before we departed. Laini came out to join us as well. Kids LOVE motorhomes. And "Aunt" Amy has tons of kid toys for grandkids and the such to make their visits even more delightful.

We took the usual parting pics, then headed down the road. This would be one of the longest days of driving for our trip. 427 miles. Destination: North Ogden, UT. My brother Rick and wife Cindy's home.

Not very far down the road, we stopped in Darby, MT for fuel. The man in the next lane filling his little pickup, name Jim, asked about our Allegro. His friend, named Shannon, had the exact same motorhome. Shannon lived just a couple blocks from the gas station. Jim asked if we'd drive by Shannon's house and honk and say hi. We were totally game, got directions and headed off the highway to find Shannon. It took a few driving around moments, and we were about to give up when I saw the Allegro in a back yard. The door was wide open, but I never saw Shannon. We stopped and honked a few times. No one came out, so we ventured on our way. I expect Jim talked to him later about it, and I imagine Shannon admitting he heard someone honking, but didn't go investigate.

I-15 in Montana is a nice drive. The road could use a little attention, but nothing terrible. The terrain is not like the most beautiful in the world, but still has a sweet attraction. I enjoyed the jaunt very much.

Heading down into Eastern Idaho, we came to what was much more familiar terrain, especially from Pocatello south. I lived in Utah for around twenty-six years, so that part of Idaho was not uncommon to explore. We loved visiting Yellowstone and Grand Tetons. Many years earlier, I had a friend named Gonzo attending Idaho State University in Pocatello.

Just a fun sidenote, Gonzo's apartment had only one door in and out. He was out of food, so we brought him a whole bunch of food, much to his surprise and amazement. He didn't have a phone, (this was long before cellphones), so we couldn't even tell him we were coming. When we got there, I was even more amazed myself. All he had to live on were some dry beans to cook, and a box of cornbread mix. That was it. Even in my poorest days, I've always had some food in my fridge and cupboards. Nope. That was it. Empty fridge. Empty cupboards. Just beans and cornbread, so our coming was better than winning the lottery. Well, maybe not that good, but it was wonderful to bless him with so much. He thanked us muchly for all of it, except the peas. He didn't like peas, canned or otherwise. We could take those back home with us.

While there, he mentioned some obnoxious people who came to his apartment. Not folks he knew. Maybe salesmen or Mormon missionaries. Perhaps Jehovah Witnesses. I really don't remember. What I do remember is offering a solution. I told him to put a sign on his door saying, "Please use other door." His friends and family would know that was the only door. Others not familiar with that part of the residential house turned apartment would walk around looking for the other door that didn't exist.

Years later, I put the same sign on my Winnebago I lived in for a couple of years. It had only one door. Not even a door by the driver – just the one to enter the living room of the vehicle. So, I put the "Please Use Other Door" sign as a lark. I could be funny seeing people come to our door, see the sign, walk around the RV and wonder, what gives?

Back on I-15, the further south we went, the more familiar surroundings for me. I'd played basketball in high school against the Intermountain Indians in Brigham City. I'd been to the best pie shop in the world in Willard or Perry, UT – I don't remember which. We got much of our fresh produce from the many fruit stands along the way. We passed Willard Bay, a freshwater bay attached to the Great Salt Lake. It even freezes over during the winter.

The mountains crowd the interstate for a spell, then open up, inviting everyone to the Ogden Valley. My brother Rick and Cindy live in North Ogden. When I was a kid, North Ogden was considered farmer country. We used to joke that the kids at Weber High rode their cows to school, and the richer kids road their tractors. It ain't that way no more. Now it's some of the most prime real estate in Weber County.

Rick and Cindy have a beautiful home on the gradual hillside down from Mount Ben Lomond, now just part of a large neighborhood. Cindy's mum lives in the mother-in-law suite on the lower level. For you flatlanders, mountainous zones like Utah have lots of houses built on the side of the mountain, so the front of the house might look like a standard two-story, but if you walked around the to the back, you'll find a lower level that has a outdoor entrance and is not really a basement. When they had their house built twenty years earlier, they were one of the only houses at the top of the hill. Now tons of houses continue on up to the foothills of Mount Ben Lomond.

They built the home when Rick owned a plumbing business. Done climbing under houses in crawl spaces and the like, Rick's career as a plumber moved onto consultation that had nothing to do with plumbing. COVID moved his office into his home. Cindy works in one of the county offices. Now empty-nesters, they get to see children close by and play with the grandkids. Their youngest gave birth to her first just before we got there.

The first rule of order for any visit is where to park the monstrosity. Rick and Cindy have their similarly sized motorhome on a specially added slab next to the garage on the front side of the house. Per Rick's instruction, we could have left it on the street. This would be the first home we visited that we slept inside rather than in the RV. Still, I preferred having our old, but precious motorhome parked not on the street if we were not going to be staying inside. He made room on his large driveway, and we had not only a little better security, but an extension cord that didn't cross the sidewalk.

Rick and Cindy are barbecue royalty, so we were fed non-Mexican fare, not that we were in any way yet tired of the South-of-the-Border cuisine. Amy and I just took note for our own private trip survey as we enjoyed their barbecued chicken.

Rick's an avid golfer. He also coaches basketball, first the boys at our high school alma mater, St. Joseph's High School in Ogden, then took over the newly started girls B-ball team. He has a keen eye for sports. Just about every time we get together, he shares something he's observed that would have gone completely over my head.

One time, during a family reunion in Oregon, he noticed how my grandson ran – smoothly. His head hardly bobbed. He would have been perfect for track, including hurdles. I shared that with my daughter when we returned her son.

He knew the Utah Jazz would not win it all this year. Though they'd been the winningest team in the NBA this year, he did not see the team comradery and depth to take them through the play-offs. In pro sports, the play-offs basically start a new, very short season. They may jockey for position for home court advantage and all that, but the last place team can (and has) won it all when the playoff games were over. In professional sports, only one team finishes the season happy each year.

Their home is one where the TV is on all day, yet nobody really watched it the entire time we were there. What was on? Golf. Just golf. Both days. All day.

When we were much younger, Rick hoped he would be able to become the golf pro at one of the local courses. I play a little golf, but have never taken advantage of playing alongside my brother who would completely skunk me. Still, I'd leave with a much better understanding of the game and what to work on. Maybe next visit.

The next day, his son Andrew came to visit for the weekend. Andrew is in low 40's. He has downs syndrome, and is such a delightful young man to know. He LOVES music, especially Garth Brooks, and enthusiastically played for us some Garth on his phone.

I don't see Andrew very often, now even less with our distance of miles. I moved from Ogden to Washington in 1997. He still lives with his mom in Salt Lake most days. Despite the distance, Andrew and I continue to have a special connection when we do get together.

Many years back when he was nine or ten, we went to the park. Then, I put him on shoulders to carry him up the hill back to his mother's home. He was more than elated the entire trek. Though quite a bit younger then, I still needed to do a fair amount of huffing and puffing to get up the sidewalked slopes with my pudgy nephew. It was worth it so much more than I ever could have measured. He continues to remember that day and that has connected us throughout the years.

Earlier in the day, Amy and I had a couple errands we would have liked to get done. Rick was good to lend us his truck. Thanks Rick.

While out and about, I got a call from my bestest friend, Rob, who lives south of Salt Lake. He came up to Ogden with a Catholic priest named Father Gally. It was Father Gally's birthday, and they were having a small adventure, so called and invited us to join them for lunch. How delightful!

We dined at Rainbow Gardens, at the entrance of Ogden Canyon. Heartily recommended. Surprisingly, it has not changed much since I moved to Washington. That's not to say it has not changed – it's been through some major reconstruction. When I was a kid, we went there to swim or bowling. They had two pools, one indoor and one outdoor. Being snowy Utah, the inside pool was the only one locally where we could swim during the winter.

Then, they took out the bowling alley and turned it into a mini-mall of small boutiques. The indoor pool became a well decorated and managed store selling schtuff you'd typically only buy as a gift for someone back home. Still, it's total fun to go down into the deep end of the pool to see chimes, air spinners, cutesy cards, overpriced stuffed animals and the like.

What used to be the game area for pinball and making little medallions with your name on it became the dining area for a very pleasant restaurant. Everything I've ever had there was good. No complaints at all, and that's so rare nowadays.

We dined, celebrated Father Gally's birthday, and took some pics before parting company.

Rob is a lifelong bachelor whom I will talk about more in the next section. For reasons I cannot discern, he came to see me though we'd talked about me coming to stay at his home after Rick and Cindy's. Rob loves to shop. With no one else in his life to curb his shopping habits, he is the consummate packrat. In turn, he also keeps eyes out for bargains on huge shoes. I wear size 17 shoes. He presented me with three pairs of shoes and later a pair of flip flops because I mentioned after we left Sequim that somehow I'd left my sandals home. Two of the shoes were leather slip-on boots, and one New Balance trainers. Very light and good to wear.

We shared a closing prayer and parted company for the day. Amy and I finished our errands at Walmart, including some hair schtuff for her, then returned to Rick and Cindy's for barbecued steak and baked taters. Yum!

Rick also gave us a tour of their motorhome, a thirty foot, '97 Pace Arrow. When Amy and I were shopping for a motorhome, she insisted on getting one without slide-outs. She'd heard that they were one of the first things to break-down on an RV. Rick stated otherwise and extended his living room. Very nice, not that Amy and I went, "Wow! We screwed up." Not at all. We are still very pleased with our Allegro, but someday when we upgrade to a newer model, perhaps we won't be so offset by slide-out options. We'll see.

As you surely know, traveling changes a person's regular habits. For me, it probably changed how much water I'd consumed that day. As we settled in for the night, I went to lay down and suddenly felt like the whole room was spinning. Total vertigo – a condition I'd never encountered before, and for that matter have not had since. Not sure what cause it, but I didn't have my morning cups of coffee and ran around with Rob and Amy for some hours. None of that seemed uncommon, but I could not lay down to save my life. I sat in a rocking chair in our bedroom, sipped water for over an hour and let my equilibrium return to normal. I tried laying down at one point. Nope, not ready, so back to my chair. The next time I tried, my body settle down and I could sleep. Weird!

SATURDAY, JUNE 26TH

Departing Rick and Cindy's with the usual parting pics taken, we headed south to Rob's in Copperton, UT.

Copperton is a unique little town. It was originally built to house the copper workers working the Kennecott Copper Mine. It was quite a ways away from the metropolitan Salt Lake area. Very separate. Kennecott is still very much digging up more copper, but as the Wasatch Front develops more and more, Copperton is practically touching South Jordan. I'm sure it's going to be part of the metropolis within the next decade.

Rob bought his house out there like twenty years back. I've stayed with him from time to time. He used to describe it as like the Avenues, (in Salt Lake), but without the crime. Nothing fancy. Just comfortable, like an old pair of slippers.

The other notable was, in case you didn't know, the TV show *Touched by an Angel* was all filmed in Utah. The last program was filmed in part at the small, white painted church across the street from Rob's house.

The streets of Copperton are even narrower than Hamilton, plus they do have curb and gutter, so when you try to part a large vehicle, it takes up a lot of room.

Actually, I was totally stupid at first. We got to Rob's before he got home. I looked out back of his place which has an unusually large parking area and saw that we could park our 31' RV, but getting there was another problem. I tried and failed completely, even damaging a city water meter plate with the heavy back tires. So, I parked on the street, but the gutter was so deep that it would be more than usual to balance. My old rig doesn't have any automatic levelers. Those wouldn't be out for another decade. We just drove up on stacked boards. I had to use every board in my arsenal to halfway level it.

Rob was a bit perturbed at our parking job. C'est la vie. We go back to mid-teen years in the early 1970's. Not the first time we irritated one or the other.

The best thing about Rob is that he LOVES to socialize, and he loves to be the host. I have never met another person like him. Unlike moi, Rob keeps his relationships alive year after year. Again, being a lifelong bachelor, everyday can be a new chance to go see someone he hasn't seen for a spell.

He's been a Respiratory Therapist for decades, working in various hospitals around the Greater Salt Lake area. Did I mentioned he's a packrat? He has at least half a dozen cars. I think only two of them are in service. He becomes very attached to his vehicles and hates to let them go.

So, Amy and I loaded into his truck and cruised around the valley. He was the consummate tour guide. I'm serious. He pointed all over the place as we drove, telling about who lived where, experiences he'd had with them, places they'd dines, etc. It seemed like the entire valley was under construction – there was so much new building. Rob told us about the good, the bad and the ugly battles that ensued to build this or that.

Amy and I used to enjoy watching the Dry Bar Comedians. You can download the app on your phone and project to your TV. They changed their app a bunch, a couple/three months back and now we don't watch their schtuff, but the year before our trip we enjoyed many of their comedians' concerts. All programs are performed on stage in Provo, UT. They're all stand-up comedians and their show has to be clean, no foul language, etc. I get so tired of the foul language that so many comedians think they have to use now. Just using vulgarities is not comedy. So, we treasured the Dry Bar.

At Rick and Cindy's, I checked and found they had a show that evening, so we called Rob and arranged for all three of us to go. Fun, warm ride to Provo.

I'd not mentioned this, yet, but for whatever reason the weather was never that hot. It's late June. We're heading into places where temperatures should have been at least in the nineties. Nope. Mostly seventies and a few eighties.

Meanwhile, while we're in Fruitland and Hamilton, a heat wave hit home in Seattle and our home in Sequim on the Olympic Peninsula like none before. I understand coastal Washington has never hit 100 degrees in recorded history. Never. For two or three days, the temps exceeded 100. Our kids called from home complaining about the heat. We advised them to turn on the AC – something I don't think we'd ever used, but don't forget to turn it off after the heat wave abates. I didn't want an extra hundred bucks added to my electric bill.

The drive to Provo was the warmest weather we'd yet encountered and it wasn't that hot.

Finding the Dry Bar Theater in downtown Provo, we were pleased to see Angel Studios. I expect you've at least heard of The Chosen, the fan-funded, multi-season show on the life of Jesus, His Apostles, and the others living alongside Jesus at that time. I love the programs and have seen all of them many, many times.

I support the ministry, and if I made more money, I'd support them all the more.

The façade outside the studio and theater have huge, black and white pics of the main cast members. It was very personal to me to be closer to a program I have treasured and has been so close to my heart these last two years.

Amy and Dave Outside Angel Studios, Provo, UT

When you buy Dry Bar tickets, they offer you $25 or $30 tickets. For an extra five bucks you get premier status. It doesn't mean you get in before anyone else. It doesn't mean there are seats reserved up front for you. It just means you get popcorn and a soda at the concessions. That's it. You still have to grab the best seat you can from what's left. Rob told them we'd bought premier tickets and the usher didn't shrug, but you got that impression. When we got our food, Rob ordered two sodas. We also found seats in the balcony that gave a good view of the stage. Amy's only 5'2", so sitting back in a crowded theater can be less than the best for her. The opposite is for me. I'm quite tall, so feel sorry for most people who sit behind me in most theaters.

We were treated to two comedians that night. Unusual. One man who works there named Seth Tippette opened the show with a ten-minute routine. He's an inch or so taller than me, so tells a lot of tall people jokes. I could relate.

Brad Bonar was the headliner. He'd performed there before. This time, I think he tried to see how far he could stretch the 'clean humor' line in the sand. Not that he was crude, but touched on topics he likely avoided in his earlier performance. Still fun. Nothing overtly crude or nasty. We enjoyed his show very much, and got pics with both men after the show.

Leaving the theater, there was a large canopy set-up across the street. Still daylight, they were singing karaoke. COVID is still being dealt with, so someone set up for karaoke outside where no one had to wear masks. We enjoyed listening to a bunch of singers, some good and some bad, of course. That's just part of karaoke.

One very young girl sang a song from Frozen. Amy sang one of her favorites as well, toned down with the children there from what she might have sung in a bar. Our own Dry Bar karaoke.

Rob explored the stores and bought some pastries. We stayed till dusk, then headed to the **Strap Tank Restaurant**. Very fun place, and again really good food.

Quite some years back when Rob and I were young men, we were eating at an *Arctic Circle Drive-In Restaurant* in Salt Lake. They screwed up Rob's order. He complained and nothing was done. Then, a girl came up offering Brach's peppermints. Rob reminded her that his concerns for his food were not addressed, not meanly. No yelling or anything. It's *Arctic Circle*. Not the best nor the worst. Cheap food.

Then Rob told her that we were Secret Shoppers, but not just any Secret Shoppers. We were called the 86er's. That's what we did - go around and evaluate the restaurants in the area, then write an official report on each one, oftentimes for publication. This was long before online comments and ratings. From then on, whenever Rob and I went out to dine and the food was substandard, we'd look at one another and say, "This looks like a job for the 86er's!"

The *Strap Tank* would've passed with flying colors.

Rob told me the original restaurant is in Springville, UT, south of Provo. The owner went the extra mile to make it very, very special, designing it after the original Harley-Davidson factory. I haven't seen it or eaten there, but will make a point to next time I'm in

Utah. In 2004 I was able to tour the Harley factory in York, PA.

Rob, the perpetual connoisseur of restaurant fare, including the brewskis, paid for an elaborate feast for us. Amy picked out a Strap Tank T-shirt to take home.

SUNDAY, JUNE 27TH

The next day, Sunday, we were able to attend the Lifeline Community Church in West Jordan, UT. I don't know if it's part of a denomination, or all by itself, but I do know it follows patterns and traditions of about a dozen or so Christian denominations including Calvary Chapel, Nazarenes, Foursquare and others. The services could be readily interchangeable with nothing added or left out. I'm told by my pastor that lots of such churches come from the Armenian movement of the church – hence the strong and clear similarities. Makes me wonder why they don't stay together as one church in Christ?

The building makes you stop and wonder if you're in the right place. There's a big, nicely designed sign, so you know you're there, but the exterior is very industrial looking brick. The surrounding businesses and ongoing construction add to that effect. Still, the pastor, Dr. Bryan Hurlbutt, greeted us before we entered. Lots of love in his personality when you meet him. He's more of a teacher than a preacher, not that his sermon was void of emotion.

The worship team, a band of seven, played some great songs very proficiently. Big screen above for the lyrics as well as visual aids during the sermon and special videos as needed throughout the year. Just a guess, but I'm sure the sanctuary could seat five-hundred people without cramping anyone's style.

After the service, we headed back to Rob's, changed clothes and packed up a few items, then headed an hour and a half east of Copperton to Big Cottonwood Canyon and the Silver Fork Lodge for lunch. Quite the drive, especially when you're hungry, but still worth the wait. Of course, Rob was still the never-ending tour guide, sharing points of interest and who's who all along the way.

We told Rob Amy needed to eat. He heard but still wanted to take us to this special restaurant up the canyon. Amy gets motion sick as well. It could have been bad. Fortunately, she made it okay, even filming the windy canyon road to playback at a much faster speed.

Amy got a salad, Rob a prime rib plate, and I got a rack of ribs. Just ribs. Nothing else. No taters or rice pilaf or veggies. My one criticism of the menu. The ribs were great, but still not meant to stand alone.

Rob LOVES to pay for your meals. He'd paid for everything thus far, so when the waitress brought the tab, I gave her my card. Rob and I both practically flinging our debit cards at her. In her own words, I'd presented mine first, so she took mine.

We toured the grounds after lunch, then headed back down the winding road to the Salt Lake Valley. Whyizit the trip back always seems to go faster than the first trip up when you've never taken that road before? Always a bit of a mystery to me. I have my guesses just like everyone else, but they're still just guesses. It's not like I'd memorized the twists and turns the first time up, and it'd been many years since I'd driven up Big Cottonwood Canyon.

In case you have never been to the Salt Lake Valley of Utah, it stretches basically from Salt Lake to Ogden, (and a little beyond). Technically one could argue it goes to Provo/Orem, but they have their own lake, Utah Lake, a freshwater body of water, so not part of the Great Salt Lake.

Rising audaciously to the east is the Wasatch Front of the Rocky Mountains. All along the Wasatch Front are canyons, all carved by a river or creek. Some are grand affairs that can take you to Wyoming, like Parley's Canyon (I-80), and Weber Canyon near Ogden. Many of the canyons dead end at some ski venues. Little Cottonwood Canyon takes you to Alta and Snowbird. Big Cottonwood, south of Salt Lake, ends at lesser known Brighton and Solitude ski resorts.

Then, there are many more little canyons which have no finished roads, perfect for day hikes. One in Ogden, called Waterfall Canyon, I've hiked many times. As you might guess, it has a very tall, very nice waterwall at the top. Not much water during the dry season, but I've never known it to stop falling.

Decades back, my then brother-in-law Denis and I hiked it. We foolishly got a drink from the waterfall and had the runs, me for a day and Denis for like three days. Probably sucked down a little giardia. I'm guessing either he drank more water than *moi*, or more likely I'd built some immunities having lived in the region and drinking unprocessed water at times from springs and such when we'd camp on the mountainside. Or both.

I hiked Waterfall Canyon with my step-daughter Aubree in 2018. It was over 100^0, plus the thinner air. The best workout I'd had all decade, but we made the trek. Well worth it.

When I worked at the somewhat fancy Ogden Park Hotel in the mid-90's, guests would ask me what there was to see around Ogden. At the time there wasn't much around Ogden. It's gotten a bunch better in the last decade. I'd tell them to take a drive up Ogden Canyon – one of the loveliest canyons you'll ever find, topping off at Pine View Reservoir and the town of Huntsville. You can actually keep heading east into Wyoming. I used to go snowmobiling at a five-thousand acre spread called Sourdough, near Monte Cristo. We also used to camp beyond Huntsville at South Fork or near Causey Reservoir. Just a beautiful area to explore.

The Abbey of the Holy Trinity, a Trappist monastery was open then. I'm sad to say it has closed and the priests and brothers still living moved to another monastery. It was a striking place, and some time I'd love to tell you about the hikes I took on the mountains surrounding the monastery.

Now that I'd told you more about Utah canyons than I'd planned, back to Rob's visit. After the less than perfect night on Rob's street in Copperton, Amy and I checked out RV parks. We found Mountain Shadows RV Park in Draper, UT, south of Copperton, right along I-15, and perfect for our departure the next day. They have a sweet swimming pool for those hot days. They also have a grassy area out front with a small cascading waterfall fountain offering plenty of shady areas to rest and enjoy.

With our late search for a place to spend the night, we ended up with basically a parking spot along the entrance road. It had only electrical hookups – more than enough for our needs. Rest room and showers by the office if needed. Two other vehicles parked ahead of us, and the last place behind us remained vacant. Though kind of weird to park in the entranceway, it was also kind of nice being right by the grassy area with the cascading waterfall right out our door.

On the way to Rob's, I sighted the Camping World of Kaysville. RV sales and parts. I stopped by there for the windshield wiper we could not find at AutoZone in Hamilton. I got the exact wiper for my make and model RV. Perfect. But instead of trying to put it on right there, I waited till we got to Rob's. Oops! The part didn't fit at all. I have to deduce that the wiper arms have both been replaced since the vehicle was built. My best option would be to replace the arms as well as the wipers.

For whatever reason other than because they can screw us over and what else are we gonna do, these basically common windshield wipers were like four times more expensive than a decent pair of wipers at Walmart. I wasn't pleased to throw away forty-something dollars, but would have been around forty-two miles from Rob's to return them. As you know, when you're driving a vehicle that gets around ten MPG, and fuel is around $3.50/gallon, that's $14 or so just to drive back to Kaysville, plus another $14 to re-cover the miles back to Copperton or Draper. To my pleasing surprise and amazement, the Draper RV park was right next to Camping World of Draper. We were easily able to return the wipers there, thank You Jesus.

I have a decent cell phone. You'd think I would have checked to see if Camping World had other stores. Duh!

We refilled propane at Mountain Shadows. Seventy-five bucks.

Rob arriving, we crammed into his little Toyota to go bowling. Rob was not pleased to go bowling, but went along, then ended up having a delightful time.

It has not been that long since Amy and I had gone bowling – a few years, but we were surprised to find the bowling world had gotten much greedier. For those of you who haven't been there for some time, payment is very different. Remember how it used to be? You'd be assigned a lane or two, get your bowling shoes and go play however many games you wanted. Now it's pay up front by the hour. That includes shoe rental. $51 for the hour per lane.

We played our first game, then started the second. About the third frame, the lights went off. Our hour was over. Period. Rest of the game lost. What a crock!

This was a newer outfit called All-Star Bowling. The lanes have colored lights on them for esthetics, I guess. Each lane also has a video screen above it advertising something. Very obnoxious.

We asked about getting a beer. You have to go to the bar which is a separate room marked Adult Bowling. We expected it was just a few lanes where adults could play without children close by. Maybe they allowed smoking in there or something. The entire facility has tons of video games, prize games, mini-golf and more. Quite the recreation area, so kids would be in tow with some of the adults bowling to be sure.

Nope, we were wrong. Adult bowling has the same video screens over each lane, but they're programming is soft porn. As Christian people, this was not attractive at all, and a bit of a disturbing surprise. I enjoy having an alcoholic beverage occasionally – usually a beer. We'd had a local brew with our lunch at the Silver Fork Lodge, but that doesn't automatically mean I want porn thrust at me while I order my beer.

Perhaps ever odder, you don't take the beer with you from the bar. The doorman takes your drinks to the door then hands them to you as you leave that room. I'm sure his hands were not all that clean, plus this was still the season for COVID. For us, a strange set-up.

On one positive note, the bowling balls in that section looked like large pool balls. That was rather fun to see.

After bowling, we all headed back to the RV. Amy went to bed while Rob and I visited inside till after two a.m. It was one of the best visits of our Great Adventure. We each shared some songs including the last two I'd composed. Hugs and endearments when he left. It's always such a blessing to see my old friend, and though both of us are not really that old – both mid-60's, there's always that nagging reality in the back of our minds that this could be our last Earthly encounter. Young people with no significant health concerns don't think in such terms. I promised to keep in touch during our travels. Rob is the one person I've kept close touch with in all my years and travels and pitfalls and whatever else in life.

MONDAY, JUNE 28th

Departing Draper, we headed south along I-15, past Provo to Spanish Fork where we turned onto Highway 6 towards Price, UT. I-15 is typical interstate fare versus Highway 6 which offers a more adventurous travel. Not like a single lane dirt road up the side of a mountain or such, but it blazes through winding mountain passes. Livens up the scenery a whole bunch; not uncommon in Utah. Many highways squeeze between the never-ending mountains.

Our old motorhome with a 5.9 liter Cummins Diesel loves to cruise. On a level road, it is most comfortable around sixty-three or sixty-four mph. Down hills it will easily pass seventy, compelling me to touch the brakes well before loss of control.

Uphills are a different matter. That engine in that big box doesn't leap up the hills. It often got a bit hotter than I would have preferred, and we topped some pretty steep slopes at slow speeds.

Have you ever considered when traveling about, why a town or city developed in that spot? We followed a river for many miles, oftentimes leaving the mountain pass for wide open spaces, yet very little human development, if any at all. Then, you pass some remarkable rock formations and smaller mountains and suddenly you enter Price, UT. Why did they settle there? A mining town at one time that developed into its own community apart from mining? Probably.

Leaving nestled Price, meeting Highway 191, we were back in the mountain passes for a stretch. Then, the mountains slid away as the highway crossed a huge, barren expanse that took us to the town of Green River and I-70.

With no working fuel gauge, we refilled the tank in Green River, UT. My brother Jay in Fruitland had told me my tank was probably big enough to go many hundreds of miles – even a thousand miles. As the trip continued, I tested it, going a little further each time.

I'd reported earlier that Eric's RV Repair suggested I put two bottles of Seafoam in the fuel tank, that it might loosen the fuel gauge float. Apparently it worked, because I started seeing the fuel levels measured and appropriately dropping as I drove farther between fill-ups.

Though Moab and Arches National Park were our day's destination, there's always more to see along the way. In this case, I wanted Amy to visit the Goblin Valley. I'd been there before – the last time in 2006, yet the amazing rock formations that stretch about a mile by a mile and a half across this small valley were notably larger than I'd remembered.

It's hot and dry in the Goblin Valley in late June, though not nearly as hot as the last time I'd trekked it. No vegetation of any kind. Just red/orange rock formations all setting upon hard pack ground. It's truly an amazing site to visit.

They'd added some picnic structures and descriptive signs since I'd last visited. I'd hate to be out there during a lightning storm though the large, covered picnic area would supply totally adequate protection from lightning.

Amy and I loved touring the rocks. Goblin Valley was used for filming the Gorignak scene in Galaxy Quest with Tim Allen and Sigourney Weaver. The first time, I made a point of seeing the movie again before we got to central Utah. The ranger station asked if we'd seen the movie before we entered.

After we toured the Goblin Valley, we took a quick drive through the camping area. It has that remarkable combination of beauty and desolation. Little mountains surround it. It's both unremarkable and exceedingly attractive.

Amy and Goblin Valley, Utah

Heading back to I-70, we cruised another twenty miles or so past Green River to rejoin Highway 191, heading south to Moab.

That stretch of road is open sage brush atop red dirt. It's amazing to see as you turn south, and even more amazing to behold. Dark red rock formations appear across the open fields, getting closer to the highway the further south we drove. At some point I considered the rock could not get much darker and still be red.

We passed the entrance to Arches National Park, a few miles before Moab. We'd heard they were counting vehicles entering the park. When COVID quotas were reached, a vehicle would not be cleared to enter until someone exited.

Just before entering Moab, we crossed the Colorado River. The river has worn an outstanding swath through the desert. Tall sheer walls border the river on each side, south of Moab. I'd guess the walls are fifty to sixty feet tall, but that's just a guess. Could be taller. There's a winding, two-lane road that follows the east side of the river through the high canyon. If you watch, you'll notice some petroglyphs on one rock close to the road.

A few miles out of Moab in the that Colorado River canyon, lies Moonflower Canyon. Years earlier when I lived in Ogden, I'd bring the family down every year to camp there. At the time it was just a lovely canyon that went back maybe a quarter of a mile deep into the wall. Lots of slickrock on three sides. The kids could run wild. It also had a small parking lot out front, but otherwise absolutely no amenities. No water. No electricity. Not even a porta-potty. Pack your camping gear in, then pack it out.

Amy and I didn't explore it this trip, but I've been told it's been redesignated as a state park, so one has to pay $ to explore.

We had made reservations at Canyonlands RV Park in Moab, right on the main drag through town. We secured our RV site, then walked into downtown to explore.

The main road through town has dozens of shops, places to eat, etc. Some were still closed due to COVID even though this was the core of the busy tourist season. The restaurants that were open all had lengthy waiting lists to get seated. We put our name in at Miguel's Baja Grill. Nothing fancy, but good ratings. You'd think we would have avoided Mexican by now.

The hour plus wait let us explore the shops. Amy, who loves purple, bought a Moab T-shirt. It was summery warm, of course. Some of the blocks had misting water overhead, cooling us along the sidewalks. We rested for a moment under the thin water to cool off.

Moab had tons of new construction going on everywhere. Mostly new motels, especially on the north side of town.

Enjoying the "sidewalk patterns", we decide to not wait the hour to eat and just fix dinner at the RV. Not that much faster. We still had to walk back to Canyonlands RV Park, but certainly cheaper.

Along the way, we noticed a restaurant with lots of ice cream. Time for dessert before dinner. We shared a banana split. The dining room was packed and noisy and not a place designed for its ambience, so we found a bench outside, alongside the parking lot, to share our treat.

While eating, a family exited the restaurant, heading to their car. The teen daughter who'd just been fed and given a yummy dessert was still being snotty and rude to her parents. At that moment, Amy and I looked at one another with gladness. We'd just received complete and full confirmation that leaving Quinnlyn at home, her eighteen-year-old daughter, had been the right decision.

Chili dogs for dinner in the RV.

Canyonlands RV Park is a nice place to stay. Our travel dates had changed after I'd made reservations – to stay an extra day with Rob. Unfortunately, they did not have a spot for us to stay the next day at the RV park, so we had to make a new reservation at ACE RV Park for the second night.

TUESDAY, JUNE 29th

Rising not too early, we still wanted to make a full day of hiking and exploring through the Arches. Driving in, there was only a small line of cars. I already had my Senior National Park pass. $80 lifetime, but don't lose it. You will have to buy another one, full price.

There's always much to see in Arches, but we knew exactly where we first wanted to go. Delicate Arch.

Delicate Arch is easily the most famous landmark of the hundreds of arches, both in and outside the park. It's the orange glob on Utah license plates. It's distinct in that it rises up off the rock rather than an eroded opening under the top of a chunk of rock or an outcropping or big wall.

There is mile and a half hike, mostly uphill, to the arch. The trail is not difficult to follow, but you'll definite elevate your heartbeat and breathe a bunch more air. For folks like us who live near sea level, the thinner air makes the climb all that much harder – but still totally worth it.

Nice parking area at the start of the hike, including room for RV's. We took the parking spot where we could see our little rolling home most of the way up the first hill.

The first part of the hike passes the Wolfe cabin. One of the first settlers to the region. There's a creek that runs by the cabin, still flowing with a bit of water in the early summer. I expect it dries up for a spell before the end of the sunny season, but I could be wrong.

It's supposed to be the original cabin, but I noticed no fireplace. The area gets snowy cold, so heat would be pretty much a necessity.

Behind the cabin are a good collection of petroglyphs. They have it partitioned off so you cannot touch them which is fine, of course. Got some good pics.

Throughout Slickrock Country, there are tons of hiking trails, but some of those trails take you over bare rock where the 'trail' is not so clear. To help, there are small stacks of rocks, usually no more than a foot high, called cairns. That name always sounds like a film festival to me. For us, there were plenty of hikers ahead to follow, passing the many cairns. There are lots of night hikes to Delicate Arch. I'm sure the cairns are most appreciated then.

We came upon an elderly woman, hiking with her cane. She was trying to step off a rock onto sand, a little more than a foot down. Amy saw the situation and helped her. She appreciated the help, and said her husband was up ahead, so we continued on.

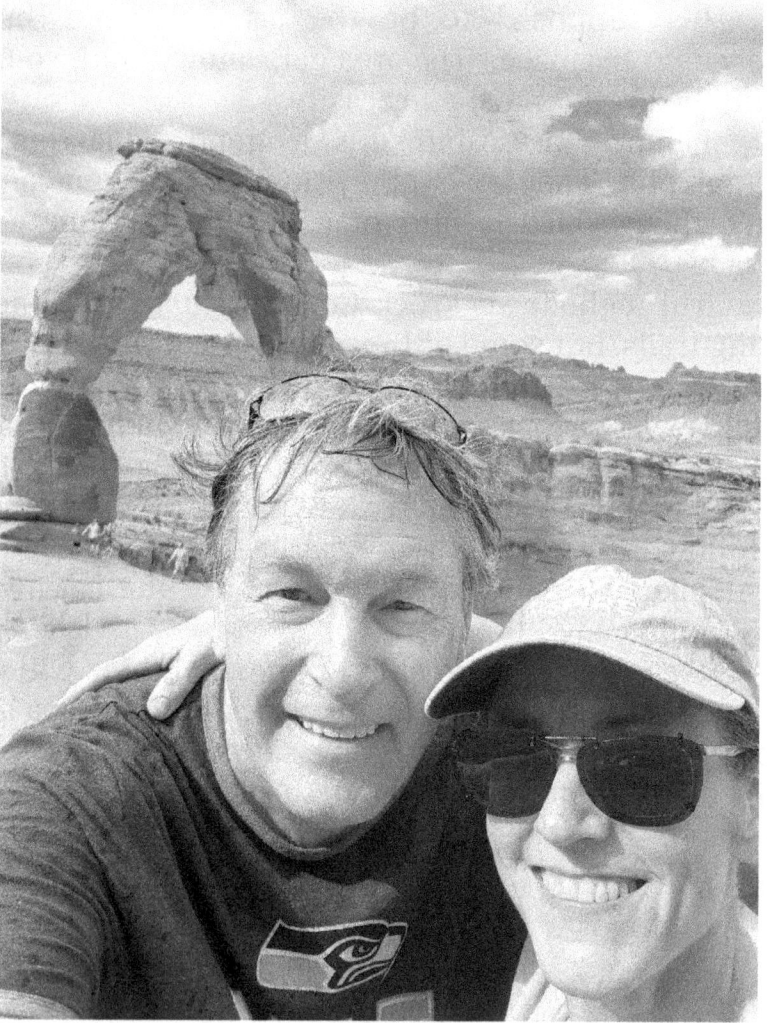

Amy and Dave Before Delicate Arch, Utah

As you approach the end of the hike, still not in sight of Delicate Arch, the trail becomes a shelf along the side of the mountain. Still ascending, some get a little nervous if they're on the outer side of the walk with a decent sized cliff below. Some hikers coming down will tell you that you're almost there.

It's always fun to reach the arch – not only at the end of an arduous hike, but also because when you see the real McCoy, it's always more awesome than any pictures can capture or convey. This was the third time I'd been to Delicate Arch. For Amy, the first time. You climb onto a shelf overlooking the arch. If you want to get a picture under the arch, you climb down off the shelf, archside, a few feet. There were lots of people there who, to my amazement, were actually being very civil and cooperative and respectful. We got in a line while each hiker had a chance to get a private photo time under the arch. The line moved quickly enough.

We got chatting with an Indian couple named Pat and Uma, who live in Connecticut. They'd been in the US for around twenty years. When their turn came up for pictures, we offered to take some for them, and they did the same for us. Very nice.

Then, as we headed away to start down, we saw the older woman we'd helped earlier. Her husband walked with her. We stopped to chat. They were named Jitu and Minal. We learned she was very afraid of heights, so climbing the Delicate Arch was a bigger challenge for her – and a bigger success. Add her advanced age and body slowing down, it was indeed impressive she made it.

As people wait their turn for pictures, the slickrock surface curves down. For Minal, it was a bit more challenging to keep her footing. Jitu, also elderly but much more physically able, offered to help her move forward, without much success. As Amy and I came by, Amy offered an arm. The woman readily accepted Amy's help and we stayed with them until they were done with their pictures.

Jitu wasn't incensed or anything, but he quipped, "You've known me for thirty years, and you trust this woman you've known for only five minutes?"

We enjoyed chatting with them the whole while. Also from India, they had lived in Maryland for some years. He had his degree in Environmental Preservation, and had worked for the World Trade Organization (WTO) for some years as they expanded their interests into preservation efforts.

We got the group of pictures they requested, and were going to head down, but there was another cliff we'd not explored. I went up, Amy followed, and we invited to help them see it as well. Again, Minal accepted Amy's help and we got a delightful view most people up there miss. Then, since we'd spent this much time together, we enjoyed the hike back down to the parking lot together, the women chatting rapidly from behind and the sober talk of men in the lead.

Jitu told of working for the World Trade Organization, then shared that he was working with a program in Maryland that does outreach to the abundance of poor sections of India. They seek some of the brighter young people, many who show signs of being leaders. They train them to become leaders, plus try to give them a moral compass to guide their adult years. There are lots of slumlords in India. They are trying to break that pattern with their program.

74

Jitu asked what I did and, of course, I told him I was a writer. He asked what I wrote and I answered mostly Christian fiction. He was amazed. He'd never heard of Christian fiction, so we talked about that for an eighth of a mile or so. He suggested I get our kids involved in making videos to promote my books. The young people know how to get the most out of our technology. I haven't taken him up on his suggestion as yet, but the year is still young. We shared more pictures when we got to the parking lot. We came upon Pat and Uma, the other Indian couple we'd met. The two Indian couples didn't know each other, of course. No biggie or surprise. It's not like all folks from India know each other all over the US, but it was still remarkable for Amy and I to have the two couples we shared the most time with on the hike originally from India and now living on the east coast.

Parting company, we headed further in the park to see the other sites. We did two other short, not uphill walks, but the Delicate Arch hike pretty much did us in. By the end of our day, we were driving by some of the sites and just taking pictures from the window.

I love exploring the Fiery Furnace. Not in the cards that day. We had to settle for the view area that gives a bare glimpse of the hundreds of fins rising from the ground.

There's a video one needs to watch at the Visitors Center, explaining cryptobiotic soil, and why it's so important to not walk on it. The ecology of the park is truly sensitive and certainly not helped by having a million humans walk around the arches every year. Staying on the trails is not just a good idea – it's necessary for the health of the foliage and wildlife at the national park.

We also did a short hike around the Devil's Garden, near the end of the paved road.

To be honest, I wish we could have spent a week there or more. There's so much to see and we barely scratched the surface.

Returning to Moab, we checked into ACE RV Park. Not as fancy or nice as Canyonlands, it would more than be adequate for the night. I make it sound unappealing, but actually they have some nice features I'd not yet found at any other RV park. They had a covered picnic area by the office, complete with a bunch of barbecue grills. The covered area is also by a kitchen and dining area which the guests may use anytime. Clean up after yourself.

The whole park is on a bit of a hill, so expect to have to level you RV when you come.

Hot dogs and potato salad for dinner in the RV.

WEDNESDAY, JUNE 30th
DESTINATION: GRAND CANYON – NORTH RIM

Departing Moab, heading south along 191, we stopped in Blanding, UT for some groceries. We knew there would be few places to shop at the North Rim of the Grand Canyon.

When planning our trip, Amy and I considered whether to go to South or North Rims. I'd been to the South Rim twice and had always sought to see the North Rim. Amy had never been to the Grand Canyon, so was game for whatever. Visiting Jay and Jenn (back on June 19th), Jay talked up how much more special the North Rim. It didn't take much arm twisting to convince us to follow his lead.

Before departing, I'd checked a bunch for an RV park. Nothing on the North Rim, and the South Rim parks were already full. I'd check over the days before we left, but no go. Nothing left but tent sites.

Boondockers suggested staying in the Kaibab National Forest. Lots of places to park a big rig without connections. That had been the plan when we departed. Then, brother Jay's suggestions changed our course. It turned out to be the best choice.

For me, and I'm sure for most people, as you drive along the highways you pass turn-offs to sites you've never been to. We had a schedule to keep but was ever sad I could not explore so many of the places we passed. Who knew when we'd be back in that neighborhood? I've never been to the Bears Ears National Monument. We would have appreciated seeing the Hopi Reservation or the Grand Staircase Escalante National Monument, all within a short driving distance. We passed through Page, AZ which is the southern tip of Glenn Canyon. If you love that terrain, my recommendation is to move there for a lengthy stretch of time just to see it all. Southern Utah and Northern Arizona really are treasure chests waiting to be opened and thoroughly explored.

Still in Utah, we left Highway 191 for 163 which has little dots beside the red line of the highway in my atlas indicating a more scenic drive. Incidentally, sometimes you have to drive quite a few miles to reach the scenic part of the drive. Also, my stepson thinks I'm old fashioned and still living in the 1980's because I use paper maps, playfully teasing me at times. But, I'll tell you, there are definitely advantages to a paper map that the electronic maps do not fulfill. It's probably better on a larger screen like my laptop computer, but when I'm traveling, I would use my cellphone to see where I was going. You really have to zoom in tightly to see many of the towns and features. It also does not alert you to the better scenic drive like a road map or atlas. My phone does a great job telling me the fastest way to get to a destination, breaking it down in both miles and hours. That's a truly appreciated feature. I use it often. Much easier than adding up the miles in an atlas. Both the atlas and the online map have their strengths. Thus, I happily take advantage of each.

Driving along this beautiful countryside with buttes and long, straight roads, Amy suddenly exclaimed, "This is where Forrest Gump stopped running!" Just south of Mexican Hat, UT in the Monument Valley. Sure enough, she was right. We didn't stop, looking for the exact spot, but she got some great pictures of the road ahead displaying the bluffs in Forrest Gump. How fun! Totally unexpected.

It was also somewhere along this road, that Amy named our old motorhome. She thought we should name it Maurice, after the man we'd bought it from who lived in Olympia, WA. The name didn't seem appropriate for our old vehicle – too French. I'd considered the motorhome to be female, like ships and such. Amy thought its personality was far more masculine.

I'd recently watched a documentary on the Bee Gees. One of the brothers was named Maurice, but was pronounced like we'd say Morris in the US. I mentioned that while our old diesel chugged up a hill. Amy perked up and said, "We'll name it Morris because it purrs when it goes up the hills." Thus, our little home away from home was christened in spirit to be called Morris.

We met Highway 150 at Kayenta, AZ. Kayenta seemed very sad to us. It's dusty. There are little houses that are barely a step up from a shack. It's very flat and shows little appeal to attract anyone to stay any longer than they need to.

We fueled up there, then tried to get something to eat. First going to Sonic, Amy headed to the rest room. It was so filthy, she refused to use it, and that's saying something because she wants the facility to be reasonably cared for. She was a wheat farm girl, so not super prissy at all. We went next door to McDonalds. They had a huge line through the drive through, but the dining room was still closed for rest room use. We wound up heading to the gas and groc further down the street. We used the toilet in the RV when we have to, but are preferentially glad to use public and private

79

facilities when available, especially for the stinkier ones. Easier to clean-out later.

I meant to take Highway 150 all the way to Tuba City, (*isn't that a great name?*), but let the whim of the moment carry me off on Highway 98 to Page, AZ. I'd never been to Page and totally looked forward to seeing it even if we were just passing through. Leaving Page, we continued on Alt 89 to Jacob Lake, then turned south onto Highway 67 – a dead-end road that ends at the Grand Canyon.

Along Alt 89 is the Navaho Bridge over the Colorado River. It's a pair of spandrel bridges overlooking Marble Canyon. There's a large parking lot, rest rooms and visitor center. I didn't notice how easily for eastbound traffic to turn into the parking lot. Probably not hard. I just didn't think to look.

The bridge also has a wide and open sidewalk for us touristas to cross the bridge, take pics and just enjoy a nice walk after hours of driving. I took a couple sweet 360^0 panoramics on the bridge.

What's wrong with our society? We can put swimming pool blue evaporation pools near Dead Horse Point, ruining the picturesque scenery. We can replace the quaint rock walls that adorn the road of a lovely canyon, in favor of ugly concrete Ecology Blocks, (talk about misnaming something), citing it's for better safety. We can build dams that control the annual flooding of riverbanks, thereby removing the biomatter that rejuvenated the banks for plant growth, leaving the banks barren and dead after a few years. So, why can't we build a bridge across the Grand Canyon? I mean, if anyone actually considered that Evel Knievel could jump across it on his motorcycle, we should have no trouble building a bridge.

(Before some of you get your panties in a wad, no, I'm not being serious about the bridge across the Grand Canyon.)

Driving south along Highway 67 towards North Rim in our 31' motorhome was a bit of a drive of faith. The Kaibab National Forest was closed to camping because of a fire from some years past. There was no RV camping available with any room to stay. The DeMotte campground was full. It was getting later in the day and we would not want to drive all that way, have an hour or so of viewing the canyon, then depart.

As it turned out, we were given no problem at all. There may not have been any camping or RV park to use, but it's free to "park" all night. Amy was a bit worried they'd ask us to move or something. Nah. I knew we'd be fine and slept soundly. Another trailer was parked beside us, following our lead, plus other RV's in the vicinity. We were in good company.

Arriving a couple hours before night, we strolled along the rim till we reached a quarter mile hike to Bright Angel Point. There are some Bright Angel things on the South Rim, but I'm told Bright Angel Point was first named by John Wesley Powell.

Amy seemed fine, but I was definitely affected by the thinner air. At 8,100 feet above sea level, it's probably the highest I've been on foot since the 1970's. The South Rim is like a thousand feet lower elevation.

We saw four young people laying on their backs with their heads over the cliff, just for the different and exciting perspective. At first glance, one might have concern for their safety. Getting closer, you could see the drop-off went down only a few feet before the real cliff of the huge canyon began.

As the sun came close to setting, stretching our shadows beyond measure, I noticed the shadows of our legs crossing the asphalt trail diagonally. Our main bodies stood against some bushes. Amy grabbed camera. It's a fun picture. Even better, my head appears to have eyes and a smiling mouth from the lighter colored spaces in the bush.

We showed the pic to a couple passing from Dallas and chatted with them for the next half hour. It was always surprising how friendly everyone can be. People we didn't know, had never met, and would never see again, stopping to chat like old friends, then moving on in life. Ships don't always pass in the night. I was surprised that they didn't try to take the same picture for themselves. Maybe they thought we'd think they were copycats – in a negative way. If they'd taken the picture first, we probably would've jumped in to get our own before the sun was gone.

THURSDAY, JULY 1st

For breakfast, Amy and I feasted on microwaved eggs, prepackaged with meat and veggies. Fun! Tasty enough, and totally American cuisine.

This day always stands out every year. It would have been my dad's ninety-first birthday if he was still here.

We spent the morning walking the Transept Trail along the Northern Rim, heading the opposite direction from Angel Bright. I tripped twice, hurting my left knee, so we had to cut the trek a bit shorter.

Making the mandatory visit to the Visitors Center, we bought a gift for Quinnlyn. She loves different types of rock. We found a colored quartzite she would like. We also bought a couple aluminum, collapsible walking sticks.

There's a campsite store near the entrance to North Rim where we got snacks and drinks. Cell phone signal was virtually non-existent for us most of the time, but there we had a bar or two and could send some texts and pics.

Heading away from the North Rim, we turned onto a twenty-mile road heading to Point Imperial and Cape Royal. As soon as you turn onto the road, there's a sign stating motorhomes and vehicles with trailers totaling over thirty feet should not take that road. Our's is considered a thirty-one foot RV, but if you measure it yourself from bumper to bumper, it's actually closer to thirty-three feet. We didn't care and continued on, not that we could have turned around anytime soon. It really would be numerous miles before we would reach an adequate place to turn around, and we figured we could make it just fine by then.

The road forks between Point Imperial and Cape Royal. I opted to see Point Imperial first – a shorter drive. It has a nice circle following that small part of the rim. For being ill-advised a drive, there was plenty of RV parking. There's a very short walk to the lookout site. We gaped in awe as usual, enjoying the magnificence of the big hole in front of us.

I also appreciated that both points are about a thousand feet lower than Angel Bright. I could readily tell by how much easier it was to breathe.

As you know, our kids just don't get it sometimes. Amy's oldest, Kyler, who's now twenty-three, stated that you go to the Grand Canyon and after half an hour you're going, "Okay. That was nice. What's next?"

**Amy Jumping Near Cape Royal
At The Grand Canyon, Arizona**

Years back, my second time going to South Rim, I had my then fourteen-year-old daughter Brenna. We'd helped a friend move from Ogden to Phoenix. I really wanted to go by the Grand Canyon again on the ride home. Brenna and I caught a few hours sleep somewhere near the main tourist areas of South Rim. Rising in the morning, we got there and walked along the amazing scenery. In classic teen fashion Brenna stated, "It just looks like a big hole in the ground."

Amy and I chatted with others there at the lookout who all took pictures on phones so both of us could be in the pics, then we headed on to Cape Royal. Imperial is nice, but I liked Cape Royal better. There's a sizable gravel parking lot. Point Imperial has more shaded parking but at Cape Royal, I was able to park close to some shade on the edge of the lot.

There's a nice walk towards the rim with side stop-offs along the way. Most notably, there's an arch called the Angel's Window. You take pics of it from afar, then continuing along the trail are led out to an observation area which crosses over the window. I tried to get a closer pic leaning over the top of the window, and only wound up scraping the left side of my belly with one of the small, desert tree branches. Here it is, over three months later and you can still clearly see the place the branch scraped me.

This outlook provides a majestic view of various canyons. The actual Grand Canyon is a ways in the distance. More people came and asked us to take pictures of them. Taking pics of a group of ten or twelve, one actually sat atop the metal fence rails meant to keep a person from plummeting to their death.

Looking down, I told Amy I could see someone's cell phone. Not true, but it was fun to play and even better that it wasn't my cell phone. Before I said that, I'd actually looked diligently for a cell phone. I minored in Photography at Weber State University. I took lots and lots of pictures with a film camera. The common practice was to always, always put the strap around your wrist when you were shooting, so if you dropped the camera, you wouldn't lose it. Cell phones don't commonly offer that same protection. I would not have been surprised to see any number of cell phones at the bottom of the cliff.

We stayed until nightfall. The plan was to stay the night up there and engage a full sky of brilliant stars. Barely a cloud in the sky. Yet, as nightfall became real, I became somewhat concerned about our welfare. The only people left there, we were sitting ducks and easy targets for any number of nefarious people from any number of directions. It became more and more clear that I would not get much sleep that night.

Eventually, I confessed my concerns to Amy. She had not considered any such danger, and after a quick discussion, we opted to head down. Dumb decision. I sit here typing going, "I'm sure we would have been fine. We should have just stayed on the mountain, even if it was twenty-eight miles from any help." Or, perhaps my discernment was spot on and I did the right thing. No way to ever know.

We drove slowly down the long and winding road that leads to your door. This was the first time I'd driven the big box at night. The connections for both driver side lights – the head light and high beams, didn't work. I could see well enough, so didn't stop. Puzzled

87

at first, it turned out to be more than an easy fix, just having to jiggle the connectors on both lights. I'd already replaced both main headlights right after we bought it and they'd worked fine when tested. Now, when they were needed, both lights decided to take the night off.

We returned to the driveway with the convenience store we'd visited earlier that day, found a secure place to park and bedded down for the night. Not as good as it should have been, but I slept a bit more soundly.

FRIDAY, JULY 2nd

We considered viewing the rim one more time before leaving, but today promised to be much fun. Heading to Farmington, NM for the night. Two of my teen grandkids were there for the summer, staying with their mum. Neither Amy nor I had been to Farmington. For that matter, and part of the attraction of taking I-40 to our eastern destinations was that that roadway had replaced Route 66. All along the interstate you'll see signs for Historic Route 66, but I'm getting ahead of myself. We still had to get there from the North Rim.

There's only one road in and out of the North Rim. Highway 67 to Jacob Lake. Retracing our travels, we also headed east on Alt 89, but when we got to Bitter Springs, AZ, we stayed on Alt 89 heading south to Highway 160 and Tuba City where we refueled. Might as well see somewhere new.

Something I'd not mentioned heading to North Rim, we were crossing through the Navaho Nation. Two items really stood out. The first were the many jewelry stands along the way, some seemingly out in the middle of nowhere. Amy wanted to stop, but I wanted to get to North Rim before dark. Uncertain how quickly we'd get there, I kept going and said we would visit them on our trek to Farmington. Leaving North Rim around 6:30 a.m., I found I'd been wrong to have not stopped. They don't keep shopkeeper's hours. This ain't Walmart or Costco. None of the stands were set up or open for business until well after we passed. Very sad.

The second item was that COVID mask restrictions and customer count restrictions were very strongly imposed at many gas and groc stations. The

Navahos don't necessarily trust the US. That certainly included the COVID plandemic, so most of them were not vaccinated and they didn't care if you'd been. Wear the mask and only X number of people allowed in most businesses at a time.

Another place we'd never seen was Four Corners – where Utah, Colorado, Arizona and New Mexico all meet together. It's not the kind of place I would have made a special trip, but we were 5.2 miles from the entrance, so of course we were going to stop and see it. Or so we thought.

Because of COVID restrictions, the Navaho Nation had closed the monument. I know not why. It's an outdoor display. Mount Rushmore was open and had a bunch more people there, but the Navahos decided to honor COVID restrictions by shutting and locking the entry gate. That was unfortunate and all, but for reasons I know not, they didn't tell you before you got there. It would have been reasonable to put signs up at junctions telling travelers that the monument was closed. Just in the few minutes we were there turning around and heading back the 5.2 miles to Highway 64, around a dozen vehicles stopped and were turned away, coming from both directions.

So, before you head that way, make sure it's open.

The roads were also an adventure. Lots of slants and shifts and other ways to make your big box bounce around. Surely the worst roads we drove on all trip.

Another fun moment of our drive, Amy was in the passenger seat looking at her phone while we were still in Arizona. She got up, came over to the couch behind the driver seat, snuggled up next to me and said, "Happy Anniversary." Apparently, we'd both forgotten it would be our third anniversary on this trip. During all of our planning and discussions and such for the trip, it never once occurred to either of us that our anniversary would be during our Great Adventure. Her Facebook page popped up a page reminiscing on three years back. Oops!

I'm equally amazed at myself. I almost never forget an anniversary.

Heading into Farmington, NM, we had reservations at Bluffview RV Park. Doesn't that sound picturesque? Bluffview? Except there's no bluff, at least not anywhere close. We were disappointed before we drove in. It's basically a gravel parking lot with RV's jammed in as tightly as they can fit. No trees. No shade, and yes, it was getting hotter in these southern zones.

Oddly, it was the only RV park that did not require me to prepay online before we arrived. It wouldn't surprise me if they'd had unhappy customers a little too regularly already.

Basically, we drove in and immediately drove out.

Checking our phones, Amy called another RV Park for possible vacancy. The man who answered was very pleasant as she explained what happened, and we were not pleased with what we found. He asked which RV park and she said Bluffview. He said Bluffview was his other RV park. Slightly embarrassing moment, perhaps, but it didn't last long. We still didn't like the park.

He checked what we needed, learning about the grandkids. He said there was a pool within a mile of the RV park, and talked us into staying at Bluffview. We parked and I went to the office. The proprietor was out, so I could not even pay as yet.

The first thing you do when you park in an RV park on a sunny day is plug into the electricity to get the air conditioner running. Thus far, I'd only had to use the 20 amp lines. My 30 amp plug had an adapter for standard 120 volt, 20 amp circuit. The adapter had worked fine thus far, so I left it on. The adapter was extremely hard to remove. Unfortunately, when I plugged in, the air conditioner tripped the circuit. We tried a few times, turning off other electrical items, but the 120V circuit wouldn't hold. I'd used the 120V plug everywhere else along the trip and even before we left without tripping circuit breakers, including my own driveway. After not even fifteen minutes of playing that game, we stowed up and headed out again.

Amy had called Moore RV Park in Bloomfield, about fifteen miles down the road. They had space and better, had a pool. We beelined there, checked in and were far, far happier with our decision. Trees covered the area. It was a very pleasant place to stay the night. Heartily recommended.

My grandkids Brenden and Karys came for their visit. They knew to bring swim gear, and had a delightful time in the pool.

I enjoyed sitting with my feet in the water. Swimming's okay, but not my favorite activity, so I'm typically glad just to hang by the pool. Brenden stayed close with me at first, but then the attraction of the cool water and the chance to drown his younger sister held too much temptation to ignore.

After the fun in the sun, we offered to take them out to eat. Karys quickly voted for a steak place – apparently her favorite. She selected the Texas Roadhouse. It's a great chain, though we'd never heard of it before that day. We told them it was our anniversary and that we were visiting our grandkids, so they came with a small cake and a bunch of staff sang a happy anniversary song for us.

Prices really were not that bad for a steakhouse. Amy and I commonly share a meal, partially to save money, but especially while we'd been traveling to keep the leftovers to a minimum. The 23-ounce T-bone looked good, but we'd have to order a second baked potato. Personally, that's my favorite part of the meal if dressed right. I'm the master chef when I prepare my baked potato for consumption.

Years back when I was working in a restaurant and private bar in Salt Lake, called Dooley's, I was working in the kitchen. I fixed myself a baked potato one time. They had those lusciously huge baked potatoes. One of the waiters saw my potato and asked if he could have a bite. Of course, it was alright. Then, it turned into a regular stop for him when I fixed my baked potato. Then, some of the other waiters saw and wanted a taste – or two. After awhile, I started making two potatoes – one for moi and one for the waiters. They enjoyed it greatly.

I'm sure it would have been no biggie for them to bring us another baked potato, but Amy and I got smaller portion plates instead of sharing. This was our anniversary. No reason to skimp.

Then, Karys stated she wanted the big T-Bone. That was almost two pounds of meat, precooked weight. We pointed that out to her, but she said, "You don't know me and steak."

Okay. She could have the biggest steak in the place. Brenden ordered a burger and fries.

We shoulda known. She ate like a bird's portion, barely making any impact on the steak. She gave most of it to her brother who'd already eaten his big burger. He didn't finish it, but he easily ate much more than her. C'est la vie. They took the rest home and I'm sure it didn't go to waste. It was still very special to get to spend the time with them, but next time.......

After the restaurant, we took them to Bolero Bowling. Remember, we'd just been to a new, modern bowling alley near Salt Lake with Rob just a few days earlier. This one was older than the hills.

Amy exclaimed, "We just returned to the 1950's." I laughed and pointed to a sign on the wall alongside the lanes. Established in 1956.

She also laughed and said, "Can I call it?"
It may have been an older place, but it still tried to conduct business like the new one in Salt Lake. You paid for your hour. When your hour was up, even mid-game, oh well. It shut down. Still weird. Who made up this crap?

We dropped off the grandkids at their mum's and went back to Moore RV in Bloomfield to enjoy a relaxing rest of the evening with Morris.

SATURDAY, JULY 3rd

Amy is much better than I am at keeping contact with people from her past, like Jocelyn and Rick in Montana whom she'd not seen for like twenty years. That's not to say I am a complete jerk or have no regard for the people of my past. Just last year I found on Facebook one of my closest US Navy friends, named Allen, from the USS John Marshall. We've had some great chats on the phone and send each other silly things to watch when it seems appropriate. We'd not had contact since 1976, so that's a long time to be out of each other's lives.

Here in Farmington, Amy contacted a friend from GRADE SCHOOL. Who still contacts friends from grade school whom they've not seen for most of their lives? Amy. She arranged brunch with Trina and her husband Reuben at Weck's Restaurant.

Weck's is a trip. Very cafeteria style. No ambience at all, but the place was just about packed. Food was good, portions were large and prices not over the top. Nothing tasted pre-fabbed like you get at Denny's or IHOP. No mystery why it was so popular with the locals.

We got to wait outside in the ever-warming sunlight. Trina and Reuben came ten/fifteen minutes later and joined us to wait in the dry heat beside the passing noise of Farmington cars and congestion.

As expected, the women chatted like they'd never been separated by decades. On and on and on. Then, inside as we were seated, I learned Reuben was a pastor, so the two of us had TONS to talk about, apart from the women gabbing about kids, family and jobs. Very nice visit and I hope to see the again.

Reuben told me that they'd never been to Farmington before he was offered to take over the church. They'd been ministering in Colorado – not too far to go. They came down for the weekend, and the Lord's Holy Spirit said they had arrived. They'd been there over twenty years and felt very much at home in their church.

I don't know what anyone else ordered. I got biscuits and gravy – one of my favorites. When I go to a breakfast place, their biscuits and gravy can be my benchmark for the quality of the food. If the gravy's not good or small portions, etc., I know not to go there again. I have a similar test for Mexican restaurants, ordering their chili verde. If it's good, it's a good place to eat. Some of the chili verde plates I've received were thin and tasteless and terrible. Told me exactly what I wanted to know.

We chatted for an hour after we finished eating. We then chatted for the fifteen-twenty minutes in the parking lot. You know how it is. The day's travel would begin our eastern migration to Joplin, MO. I'd reserved RV parks in Tucumcari, NM and Clinton, OK the next night. Nobody there we knew, so we were not in a big hurry to get on our way.

One thing I should mention here is that you often hear that you need to make your reservation at an RV park months in advance. I found that to be true only at some key locations like the Grand Canyon. Otherwise, we really had little trouble finding a place to stay, even last minute. There aren't a lot of travelers aiming for Tucumcari or Clinton, so plenty of spaces to reserve.

Heading down Highway 550 from Bloomfield takes you past Angel Peak, easily seen from the highway.

Then on to through the Jicarilla Apache Reservation and over the Continental Divide near Cuba, NM. Near Bernarlillo, 550 dumps you onto Route 66. Yup, part of Route 66 still exists.

I'd always wanted to visit Santa Fe, the New Mexico capital, but we turned instead south towards Albuquerque. It's a little farther to drive the Santa Fe route – always a consideration when driving a fuel hog RV, but this time the reason was much simpler. Neither of us had ever been to Albuquerque, either.

I mentioned earlier that I'd foolishly left my sandals at home. Rob gave me a pair of flipflops but they bugged my toes, so we toured shops in Albuquerque looking for another suitable substitute for sandals. For most of you, finding a pair of footwear is no big deal. When you're a big footed galoot like *moi* with size seventeen feet, finding shoes is always an adventure. I can find athletic shoes pretty easily, like at Ross. Sandals, dress shoes, boots and more can be very hard to find. Big 5 often has large enough sandals, but I found nothing I wanted. We even tried a tiny big and tall store with a parking lot not nearly big enough for our obnoxious rig. The owner stayed open a few minutes longer after we called him, but he didn't have what I wanted, either. We considered buying something else, but he wanted like $65 for a simple shirt. Not in my price bracket.

Eventually, we found a pair of sliders at Ross. Not my favorite, but better than nothing.

Because the cruise control didn't work on Morris, I had to keep my right foot on the accelerator, sometimes for hours. My right leg would get very uncomfortable after a spell and sometimes I had to stop and stand just to give the leg and foot a rest. Either the first or second day of our travels, I discovered I could drive much farther if I drove in bare feet. My big shoes were too clonky to let me maneuver my foot into different positions on the accelerator, whereas my foot could push down in a variety of positions from toes to heel. My most common position was the bare edge right side of the foot where it sticks out a bit, pressing down on the accelerator like I had an itch on that side of my foot I needed to scratch.

After Albuquerque, now on I-40/66, dark clouds clustered ahead, eventually blasting us with heavy rain and wind. One of those storms I imagine Jesus encountered on the Cross. I don't say that glibly. Scary, but still beautiful to behold safely within our mobile cabin.

Such storms don't last long. After you exit the storm, you see the westbound vehicles across the median and think, "Some of you don't know what you're heading into."

The clouds and rain were long gone by time we reached Tucumcari. I think I just liked the name Tucumcari. When I was scouting the maps, deciding where to stay and dividing the days into more bite-sized portions of driving, Tucumcari quickly became an attractive stop. It's not like it had any sites of interest for us to see. It's not like we would be there any longer than we had to - just a stopover for the night's rest. It's not even like the Tucumcari KOA park was anything special. It wasn't, but we still enjoyed our little stay there.

I mentioned in Farmington that I'd thus far used only the 20 Amp plug-ins for power. This site didn't have 20 Amp plug-ins – only 30 or 50, so I had to get a screwdriver and work-off the adapter. Talk about tight, it actually pulled-off the third prong. I got channel locks to pull that piece out of the adapter and just stick it in the 30 Amp side. It worked fine, but I knew I'd have to fix it soon. From there, I used the 30 Amp at all other RV parks, and bought a different adapter for parking at someone's home. I didn't replace the 30 Amp plug until we got to Amy's mum's in Julesburg, CO, still some weeks off.

At the campground, we met a young Mennonite couple named Keith and Alison. They hailed from Syracuse, NY. They were on their honeymoon, heading to Southern California. What a fun excursion they were having, I'm sure. Keith did most of the talking while she respectfully stood one step further away behind him.

We also met two teens named Pete and Grant from Alabama. They'd captured a tarantula – the first live specimen they'd ever seen. They cut a plastic water bottle in half to trap it, showed it around and I expect let it go before they went to bed, probably a fair distance from their camper.

Locked-in for the night, Amy and I watched two episodes of The Chosen, Season 2, Episodes 6 & 7, on my phone. Fun! We had Farmington leftovers from Weck's for dinner.

SUNDAY, JULY 4th

Even if we'd totally forgotten our wedding anniversary two days earlier, Independence Day was considered before we left. Not that we had any big plans or anything nor had to buy a bunch of fireworks. We just continued along I-40/66 towards Clinton, OK

Neither of us had ever ventured along this stretch of the country, though I'd checked it out on maps often. Not far from Tucumcari is the Texas border to cross the panhandle. Amarillo sits roughly due west of the middle of that little rectangle of land. The further east we went, the more it smelled like cow manure. The smell peaked when we stopped to eat at an Italian restaurant in Amarillo. The parking lot was full of the aroma. It made me wonder if there was a McDonald's close by.

If you've never driven that part of I-40, it seems like the counties are really small. I'm exaggerating, but it seemed like we entered a new county every five to ten miles. Actually, we crossed five Texas counties that day.

Just as you enter Amarillo on I-40, there are nine Cadillacs by the freeway, half buried, nose down. When I saw them, it took a couple moments for my mind to figure out what they were, and why were they half buried like that? The locals can spray paint them with whatever. Quite the Redneck Heaven motif.

We also saw right after the Caddies a semi on its side. The screech marks on the road shared part of the story. It was full of fresh corn, partially dumped out on the ground. My guess is that the semi had to suddenly veer to keep from rear-ending someone who'd dangerously slowed down to gop at the Caddies.

Further east from Amarillo, we encountered another flash storm similar to yesterday's. Maybe even worse. Also, the weather got muggier the further east we went. We don't have that kind of weather in coastal Washington State.

Another very notable difference I enjoyed in that region were the billboards for Jesus. In Washington, those are few and far between. There's one in Port Angeles right now, but that's been the only one I've seen on the Olympic Peninsula since I've lived here, and it hasn't been there that long. As we toured the Great Plains, such signs were, glad-to-say, commonplace.

We also passed a very large, white cross just out in the field, not attached to a church or any other business. I muchly appreciated it being there as a testimony for Christ.

The RV park in Clinton, OK was different. First, called the Water Zoo Campground, it was attached to an indoor waterpark. If you paid extra for the RV space, you'd save a few bucks to also use the water park. Totally optional. We had to check-in at the waterpark to gain admission to the RV spaces.

They assigned us Space 61. When we got to that site, there was a large pickup truck parked there. A similar pickup truck was parked in the space with the mobile home, so we had no trouble finding the owners. They moved the truck, but backing in Morris found the water and sewer very badly placed and not easy to hook-up. The truck owners had been in attendance and recommended we just move to another spot. That might've sounded fishy – actually it did, but they were up front, reporting that nobody had occupied Space 61 since they'd been there. Their big pickup trucks were their bread and butter, driving large trailers – even horse trailers long distances for people. They may have lived in an RV park, but I got the feeling they were doing really well financially for themselves, and glad to spend their money on things other than fancy houses.

Also, there were PLENTY of other RV places to park. I moved to Space 10 practically across the street. It was shaded and a pull through. As expected, no one came later assigned to Space 10.

As night approached, the customary fireworks resounded throughout the town. There was no laundry room, so to celebrate our nation's 145th birthday, we visited the Clinton laundromat.

Also, you'd think being a holiday, there would be something going on in town, but nope. All the restaurants were closed except McDonalds, so that's what we settled on for dinner. Yum! Maybe!

For the first time all trip, the mosquitos pressed us to remain indoors with the evening cool. Amy and I played a board game called Skull King for the first time in our protected home on wheels.

MONDAY, JULY 5th

The waterpark bathrooms were terrible. I mean the worst we encountered all trip. No ventilation, so they were hot, even in the morning. You took your shower and felt all drippy and sweaty before you got out of there. After I got dressed, I opened the door to get some air flow in there while I shaved.

We'd expected to zip right through to Joplin, MO to see Amy's cousins, Delberta and Curt. They'd been some of the most excited for us to come, chatting or texting Amy almost daily. I'd never before met them.

It's around three-hundred miles from Clinton to Joplin – maybe six hours by the slower RV, and we should have been there by mid-afternoon, but Delberta texted Amy that her daughter Johna, and son-in-law, Neil, were in Oklahoma City for the week. They lived in Alabama, and were checking out OK City housing, planning to move back. Amy contacted them and we shared a delightful Mexican lunch at Abuelo's Mexican Restaurant. I definitely give it decently high marks.

Like other Amy friends and relatives on this trip, though I'd not met Neil and Johna, like Reuben and Trina in Farmington, Neil was a youth minister and we had absolutely no problem finding great things to talk about. He even bought a copy of Patmos while sitting there in front of me. Dinner came and went, and the staff didn't give us any grief about staying another hour plus chatting. It was wonderful. Neil and I often text each other, even now.

Oklahoma City has Garth Brooks Blvd. as a freeway exit. My nephew Andrew with down syndrome whom we'd seen in North Ogden, LOVES Garth Brooks, so we took a pic of the sign and sent it to my brother Rick.

The freeway system roads in Oklahoma City could use some TLC. One ramp, the one we exited to meet Neil and Johna, was ridged worse than Ruffles. Bump, bump, bump, bump, bump, bump, bump...... on and on practically the entire U.

Okay, so after our lunch and catching-up visit, now onto Delberta and Curt's.

Nope! Not so fast. Delberta text'd Amy that their cousin Barry had just moved back to Tulsa not two weeks earlier. So, we found the home of Nicole, Barry's daughter, where we all met and chatted for another two hours. Nicole had a bunch of kids there. I don't think all were hers. She had a friend helping and her husband stayed off to himself in the kitchen cooking. Mostly Amy and Barry talked about the old days, and only occasionally touched upon present-day news.

It was a nice visit, of course, even if I had very little to add to the conversations. That's always fine. And, we were only a couple hours from Delberta and Curts by this time.

We arrived not long before dark. Curt and I figured out a very good place to park Morris, on the lawn between the curb and his backyard fence. Easy to run an extension cord.

TUESDAY, JULY 6th

Curt and Delberta have a lovely home that is barely five years old. They'd only been there a year or so. It had to be rebuilt after the F5+ devastating wall of tornado that destroyed huge sections of the city in 2011. The woman who'd owned the house had it rebuilt and lived in it for a few years, but felt like it wasn't home anymore, and sold it.

One of the first things Delberta warned us about was that COVID had increased there significantly over the previous few weeks. Nice to know, but we still wanted to enjoy the visit with them.

That ten years past torndo became the theme of our visit, especially for Delberta. Whenever we'd go somewhere, she'd talk about what as rebuilt and what the tornado left, etc.

I was actually amazed. For a mile-wide section of the main city that had been literally flattened, there was very little evidence of the tornado. Pretty much everything had been rebuilt. Then, Delberta pointed out they could easily identify the swath left by the tornado, even now. All of the older trees were gone. New growth of trees, not yet ten years old, clearly marked the borders of the damage.

They also shared a terrible story about their son Daniel. He was in high school at the time, working at Pizza Hut. The weather was terrible, of course, but he still walked to work. Somehow he didn't notice the F5 not far behind him. When he arrived at work, his manager said, "What are you doing here?" As the wind and rain and storm increased and the sirens announced a tornado, they took refuge in the walk-in fridge. A woman customer also joined them.

They took a bungee cord and strapped the door shut for a little more protection. Holding onto one another, they felt the building ripped away above them. Then, their protective box came open. The manager and woman flew away to the left. Daniel flew away to the right. Only Daniel survived of the three.

He lost consciousness. When he awoke, he had a large gash on the back of his head. As he tried to get up, he saw a dead woman nearby. Looking around, nothing was recognizable. It had all been demolished, including the street signs. Bits and pieces of the town eventually told him where he was, and he started walking for home. Hail started, about the size of tennis balls. He would be killed by the hail if he didn't take cover. He saw a sporting goods store still stood, so rushed to take cover inside. No good. Only the front of the store remained. The rest of the building had been torn away.

He soon found a five-gallon bucket and held it over his head for protection from the hail.

He now lives outside of town in Delberta and Curt's old house. They took us by there to see it, though we never got to see Daniel or his family.

Delberta also shared that as the tornado began to lift off the ground, it left all the town junk it had picked up, in the fields and farms and yards and whatever north of town. Bricks and drywall and two by fours and roofing materials and more, strung for a mile wide and a mile or two out of town. For us, there was not much to see – it'd already been cleaned up. Again, an amazing and impressive accomplishment in only ten years.

Curt had his knee replaced a couple weeks before we got there, so hung out in his recliner most of the time. Amy and Delberta chatted by the kitchen bar. They love Jesus and we were blessed to share their home. They also took us to see their church. Being Tuesday, no services happening, but they had the key, so we were able to tour the sanctuary, say a prayer and talk about Jesus. Very nice.

I love to explore, so took a stroll that morning to Walmart before Amy arose. The walk got warmer by the minute before I got home. Our mattress had been suddenly hurting my back when sleeping for no obvious reason. The walk helped it to feel better. I figured out later my back pain was caused by the New Balance shoes I'd been wearing everyday since Ogden. I've had lots of New Balance shoes. For whatever reason, these did not work as well.

Another distinction of our visit is that Delberta and Curt never cooked while we were there. Nothing. They took us to the Red Onion Café for lunch, and Freddie's Frozen Custard and Steakburgers for dinner. No complaints, of course. Both were very good. Just surprising, and they were sweet to pay for both meals.

They also went one further. They knew we were heading to Branson, MO the next two days to see two shows. They asked if we were going to see the Haywood's? We'd never heard of them, so they bought us tickets to the Thursday evening show. Very sweet!

WEDNESDAY, JULY 7th

For our last hours in Joplin, Curt had to work at 9:30, so we got only a short visit with him before he had to go. I visited with Delberta for part of the morning until Amy came in from the RV. Then, we kinda swapped places, Amy chatting with Delberta and I getting things ready to go in the RV. We left Jopling around noon, destination Branson, MO.

One notable problem traveling by RV is that it can be loud up front by the engine. Our RV has a "doghouse" between the two front seats, covering the diesel engine. In other words, it's very close to us and thereby can make conversations between seats hard to hear.

In turn, Amy suggested getting walkie talkies. Actually, I'd brought three with us, readily available to use. Her idea was to have headphones in the walkie talkies. We noticed some sizable stores in Mount Vernon, MO, so stopped to shop. Amy went clothes shopping while I explored Best Buy.

My old walkie talkies had headphone jacks, but for the smaller jacks - not the ones for conventional headphones. This Best Buy did not have the adapter from headphone to tinier headphone, nor did they have headphones for the smaller jack. The only headphones they had for walkie talkies had a proprietary connection for that brand, so I had to buy two new walkie talkies as well as the headphones. Not cheap, but also not that much.

The headphones looked like the one Agent Smith wore in *The Matrix*. Could've been the same, for all I know. Either way, it made conversations in the RV easier.

I also visited Shoe Carnival. I'd never seen or heard of one before. They had lots of sandals, but none big enough to fit me.

We continued on to Branson and the Lakeside RV Park. It has lots of trees and a beautiful lake bordering one side. The rigs are still packed in like sardines, but I'd still the park high marks.

One of the travelers helped me back in. Before leaving on our Great Adventure, one video I watched on dos and don'ts of RV life included not having a complete stranger guide you into an RV spot. This time, my first try, I didn't turn in far enough and would have hit a large tree trunk. The man stopped me. I went forward and tried again. He was wonderfully helpful and got me positioned perfectly.

With my window down, after I stopped backing, another man complimented our old Morris. I heard him wonder how much we paid for it. I called to him out the window - that he could ask how much we paid. Eight grand.

"Eighty thousand?" he asked.

"Nope. Eight thousand."

"Only eight thousand?" he checked. Really good price in his book. He loved the old Allegros.

I don't know if you're familiar with Branson, Missouri? For reasons that I completely do not understand, it's the A-1, premier, best place in the Great Plains to see any variety of shows and exhibits. Before Amy suggested going, I'd honestly never heard of it. She'd been there only once before.

It is in the northern Ozarks, so the streets often go up and down hills. It's not an ugly place, but I didn't see any scenery that explained it's growth as a "can't miss" stopover. Fortunately, it didn't matter even an iota if I knew the how or why of Branson. Parked in the park and cleaned-up to go out, we hired a Lyft to take us to the theater. We got a ride with Rick, a retired military man who talked your ear off. He took us to one place to get the tickets, then to the theater.

We had three shows to attend in Branson over two days. That night, we would see Reza – Edge of Illusion at the Branson Famous Theater. We arrived quite a spell early, so found a touristy gift center a few blocks from the theater. It had a grill. Amy and I shared carne asada fries and lemonade. We also bought some gifts for Kyler and Quinnlyn.

The show was easily as good as the reviews. One BIG thing I appreciated about his act was that it was totally kid friendly. Lots of kids there yet not made less fun for adults to watch. He had children volunteers on stage with him at times. He brought one boy on stage for his next illusion while describing that such a thing had happened to him when he was a youngster. The experience changed his life, to be sure, and he always knew to have kids on stage could also change their lives.

After he completed the illusion, he gave his "helper" a lifetime pass for all of his shows. If he ever showed up at any Reza show, he would be allowed to attend free. Pretty cool!

Our Lyft back to the RV park was with Jeff who was totally non-talkative and drove almost recklessly. Glad that we made it safely.

THURSDAY, JULY 8th
Branson, Day 2

This trip had more than its share of good surprises, like Trina and Reuben in Farmington, NM, Neil and Johna in Oklahoma City and cousin Barry in Tulsa. This day I got to see the daughter of my pastor from Ogden Calvary Chapel. I'd attended that church in the late 1980's. Shalom lives in Springfield, MO, seventy-one miles from Branson. She drove down the forty-four miles to Branson with her friend Kendra. We met at the shopping mall near our RV. What a delight! I'd not seen her since she was like fifteen years old. Shalom was still in refular contact with my second daughter, Steven, who gave me the contact info to contact Shalom.

Shalom was sooooooo excited. When she saw me, (tall people always stand-out), she came racing up and gave a welcoming hug. I was amazed. Now in her forties, her face didn't look that different from last time I'd seen her. Readily recognizable. Amy and I only had the morning before our first show, so we strolled and chatted, as expected, catching-up on a bunch of years. We dined at the Saltgrass Steak House, then the usual pics outside by a fountain. She wanted to see our motorhome, so drove us there. The only way it could have been better is if I could've played a few songs for her on guitar. She said she would have loved that.

Actually, COVID helped bring us together. Reared in the church, she had not attended for some years. Then, Steven told her about me playing worship songs online for church services. She checked us out, and was deeply touched to hear some songs that she used to sing as a young person. She also was blessed to see one of

111

the other church leaders from her youth, (*moi*), much older of course, but so what? We still share bits of life these last few months, now that our life's paths have crossed, and intend to keep that alive for the coming years.

We should've asked them for a ride to the theater. Instead, we called for another Lyft to attend the matinee show called Jesus, at the Sights and Sounds Theater. I'll tell you, as a stage production, it was as good as anything you'll ever see on Broadway. The props were amazing. I don't know how they were able to store them all and still get them on stage in exactly coordinated, timely action. The stage technically wrapped around the audience a full 180^0. There were projection screens on stage and behind the stage to add to the effects. The characters were good, and the story was good. They had live animals on stage, and sometimes literally up and down the aisles. Roman soldiers on horses rode right past my aisle seat. It really was a remarkable and enjoyable performance.

Amy and Dave Outside Sight and Sounds Theater, Branson, MO

Then, as soon as we were done seeing Jesus, we had to order another Lyft to take us to the Clay Cooper Theater to see The Haywoods. Delberta and Curt had seen them many times and bought tickets for us to go.

In case you've never heard of the Haygoods, they are a family of performers – five men and their sister who's the baby of the family. They've literally been performing in Branson for around thirty years, so many have seen them literally growing up on stage.

I had never heard of them. Their name sounded like country music – not bad but not my favorite. Amy would have liked country much more than myself. Then, they played a variety of genres. Only one country number in the set. The lead guitarist entered the theater suspended upside-down on a cable sloped from the back of the room to the stage. He played his guitar as he hung upside-down to enter the show.

Their sister played a beautiful piece on the harp. They all sang really good harmonies. The show never lagged and I would gladly go see them again.

For dinner, we picked up some quick food at Walgreens, next door to the theater. Probably our worst meal of the entire trip.

FRIDAY, JULY 9th

Leaving Branson, we headed south to Arkansas. Arkansas has stood as a longtime, personal goal for me. It has been the one and only US state I'd not yet been in. Amy had been in Arkansas a fair number of times, but I'd been all around it, yet never made it. One of my favorite Christian performers, John Michael Talbot, lives in the Ozarks and has a retreat center. My brother John has been to one of his JMT's retreats and got to meet him.

We let the GPS guide us to the Little Portions Hermitage. Good thing we used the GPS. It's at the end of a two-mile dirt road. When you're lumbering along in the big box, you keep wondering if you're going the wrong way. Amy knew that could not be the way, and I pointed out it was a retreat center – a place to get away from the world, so we were probably still going the right direction.

Arriving, we saw only two nuns there and no one else. There were signs directing us to leave them alone – that it was something of a cloister. One nun did greet us and told us where we could go explore. They had a golden lab mixed dog named Samson who was quite glad we were there.

Entering the building, we were blessed to be able to visit the sanctuary. Beautiful place to stop and praise Jesus, feel the presence of His Holy Spirit, and just absorb His love and blessings.

We didn't stay long. Our next destination, Topeka, KS, beckoned us.

It wasn't until this day that we passed countless corn fields, tall and green with corn. As I drove and saw the miles and miles of corn fields from our little highway vantage, I became more in awe of how much food that land produced. And that was just the fields we could see from the highway. I knew there were far, far more fields, full of corn, that I could not nor would ever see. It amazed me deeply.

I also enjoyed the increase of Christian billboards. They had various messages. All pointed to Christ Jesus.

Topeka, the capital of Kansas, is where Amy's Aunt Lana lives. Now eighty years old, you'd expect an older, frail being, but she's as perky and energetic as I've ever seen her. Well, her mum who died a couple year back, did live to reach 101.

Lana lives in a condo, so there's no place for our big motorhome to park. We made reservations at Crossroads RV Park. It's a bit towards the south side of town. Nothing special at all, but fine for what we needed. We would be spending by far most of our time at Aunt Lana's and with her family. There's a Super 8 motel in front of it, so easy to miss the sign. The owner had just moved into a larger, newer trailer about a month before we arrived. She told me that most of the people there were long time residents. The fifth-wheel right next to our spot had a large, upright propane tank to hook into. They were going no place anytime soon.

Aunt Lana picked us up and would drop us off there at the end of the night. Amy and Lana's cousin Margaret also drove down from Lincoln to stay with Lana. She was a career jail worker who still worked for the Nebraska Corrections.

Lana's best friend Gwen also joined us for dinner and games. Older or not, she was still a shameless flirt.

Lana's son Ron, wife Janelle, and his family soon arrived. Ron is a fire chief in Topeka. I'd met Ron at the one-hundredth birthday party of Lana's mom, ie, Amy's Grandma Emily. We got along well right off and shared a good chat about my books and God outside the house. Glad to again see him and his family, we feasted and joked and gathered around the table, playing a card game called Code Names.

Later, Lana took us back to the RV park. That night, around 2 a.m., the wind started howling mightily and rain poured down hard. Amy awoke me, all scared there would be a tornado. After Delberta's ongoing talks about the Joplin tornado, Amy was a little more scaredy cat. She'd grown up on the Great Plains, so tornados and huge hailstorms were part of her upbringing.

She awoke me. I was not nearly as worried about the storm or twisters as she which didn't stop her from telling me we had to have a radio app on our phones so we would get the news. So, I'm groggily trying to download some weather apps and radio apps. I even offered to park under an overpass.

Against my nonchalance, she stressed that I'd not grown-up here, and didn't know what life was like in tornado country? Where was the shelter? Should be take cover inside the motel? I didn't know and actually went back to sleep as soon as she was satisfied it was just a passing storm.

The next morning, Amy felt at least a tad embarrassed for getting so scared overnight. Then, she looked out the window and declared, "See? The trailer next to us with the huge propane tank even packed up and left because of the storm."

I pointed out with a bit of amusement that the trailer and propane were still there. She was looking out the wrong side of our RV.

Somewhere around this time, Quinnlyn told her mum that a black cat had followed her home. Amy made it clear we were not taking another cat. Our cat Cooper was old, but still with us. As of the writing of this book, Cooper finally passed away, having used all of his nine lives and a few more I'm sure he stole from other cats.

SATURDAY, JULY 10ᵗʰ

It was Janelle's birthday – they never did say which one. Ron and Janelle were coming for breakfast. Lana prepared mimosas to toast Janelle when they arrived. For the first time in my life, I cooked both bacon and eggs on a BBQ Grill. It took awhile, but they turned out really good.

We played games, including two-on-two badminton without a net. We'd come to Topeka a day earlier than originally planned because Ron and family were about to start their own vacation. That Saturday afternoon, they said their good-byes to head home, finish packing and catch a plane.

Lana discovered a dinner theater that evening at Topeka Center. She called and made reservations for the four of us, (including cousin Margaret) to see The Music Man – personally one of my favorite musicals. I've seen the movie countless times. It would be fun to see the changes needed to adapt it to the live stage.

Being latecomers, we were shown to a table literally at the back of the room. We were also right next to the sound board and engineers. No complaints, I assure you. The room accommodates you wherever you sit.

The opening train scene is amazing. They were small time, just sitting in a cluster that actually looked a bit weird until the music (and make-believe train) started, then they pulled it off very well. Much fun!

The actor who played Professor Harold Hill, the main character, had his microphone popping off every now and then. I have to tip my hat to him. He never hedged for a second, or dropped out of character, or whatever. He kept reciting his lines, or singing like all was well, and actually though it was obvious when his mike failed, the room was small enough to still hear him.

I asked the sound man about it during intermission. He answered with a little exasperation that they were already taking care of it.

The woman who played Marian the Librarian had an exceptional singing voice. She was perfect for the role.

After the show, with the long summer days, Lana drove us around Topeka to show us some of the local sites and talk about her life there, houses she lived in, places Amy had visited, the state capitol building, etc. Now for her age, you'd never guess Lana was eighty – until she got behind the wheel of a car. At that point she turned into an old woman. Just the right mix of white knuckles and nails bitten, right until she drove us back to the RV.

SUNDAY, JULY 11th

Lana does not attend church regularly. She used to attend the Unitarian Church, but that had been some years back. Still, she was most accommodating and said she would take us to a church. We had no idea where Lana would take us, but she drove to one of the oldest Presbyterian churches in the state. It's a large and stately church.

We entered, being greeted by elderly women in the corridor. To her surprise, two of the women there knew Lana – one her neighbor at the condos. We made our way to the sanctuary. Lana's friend Gwen whom we met our first night, was already there. I don't think it was her regular church, either. She just came perhaps to support her friend.

Now you had to be there. It was delightful. They had a new pastor, from Kenya, named K. O. NooNoo. I don't know how long he'd been there, but I'm guessing not more than a few months.

Notably, when we entered, we were surprised to see Dr. Suess pictures all over the public areas of the church besides the sanctuary. Not what I was expecting to see. The new pastor was using a Dr. Suess book each week for the theme of his sermon. Most interesting. Our week, he taught on Horton Hatches the Egg.

As the service began, he put on a blue Horton hat, complete with elephant trunk brim. He called all the kids to the front, and told them the story of Horton Hatches the Egg with a bit of a Christian flavoring thrown in. Then, his sermon used the lessons for that book as he taught on I Peter, Chapter 1 – without the Horton hat.

After the service, Lana kind of wanted to slip out quickly, but Amy and I were more than glad to share the time with the people there. We had coffee and some baked goods. We met the pastor who'd again donned his Horton hat in the social center. Lana's pretty liberal, so these conservative Christians probably rubbed her a little, but honestly it was a nice stay, I think even for her. If anything bugged her, she kept it to herself.

We left there to have brunch at Lana's home, then headed out on the town. Margaret had to get back to Lincoln to prepare for her workday tomorrow.

Lana plays flute and piccolo with the Topeka Santa Fe Band. They had a concert in the park that late afternoon. In the meantime, we headed to the zoo. They'd built a lovely Japanese garden just outside the zoo that she wanted us to see. Then, we took a very quick tour through the zoo, mostly seeing the giraffes.

Heading to Gage Park, Lana and the band played a dozen-odd songs. Amy and I took seats on the front row. Ron's son Thomas and his family came to hear Grandma play, seated on the back row because of their baby. It started raining, and Ron's son Thomas brought me an umbrella. I was surprised by the offer and did not realize it was Thomas until after the concert was over.

There were a bunch of young girls from a local dance studio who would dance with two of the band numbers. Their teacher also did a baton twirling exercise between songs. Because I didn't know where the umbrella came from, I gave it to one of the dance studio girls seated next to me after it started to rain. Amy and I moved from front row to shelter under one of the huge trees. When I learned after the concert the

122

umbrella came from Thomas, I had to go retrieve it from the dancer. My family teased me, of course, for not recognizing Thomas.

Another very fun surprise to the concert – a butterfly just LOVED the conductor and kept landing on his back. The mostly black wings totally stood out against his white shirt. Perfect contrast. It would land for awhile, take-off, then come and land on his back again. For a short spell, another similar butterfly joined in, landing in the hair of one of the clarinet players, seated front row before the conductor. I'm sure she noticed the insect but kept playing like it wasn't there.

After the rainy concert, we dried off at Applebee's for dinner. In one of those "small world" moments, the restaurant set right next door to the dance studio for the girls we'd watched perform. Many of them also came in for dinner while we were there.

As I mentioned, we'd come to Topeka a day early. Even then, we'd planned on leaving that day, but the people we were going to see in Lincoln were not available for another day, so we stayed in Topeka. It was time very well spent.

MONDAY, JULY 12th

Even being our last day in Topeka, eighty-year-old Aunt Lana was not going to pass the time passively. Always a go-getter, she invited Amy to attend her Tai-Chi class, then go get pedicures. I stayed back at the RV park. I'd seen a laundromat a couple blocks down the street, so got our clothes washed.

Back at the RV, Amy texted me that the pedicure place was closed Mondays, so they went out for Thai food. Then she asked, could I get to the State Capitol in the next twenty minutes – ie, be there by 1 p.m.? I did my best, but still couldn't make it in less than half an hour. Lana knew the guided tour of the Capitol started at 1 p.m.

We parked in an open parking lot a couple blocks from the Capitol building. Even then, with COVID crap, we had to figure out how to enter the building. What's funny is that Lana walked to the building faster and with more verve than either Amy or myself. We had to push ourselves to keep up.

Finding the entrance, we headed up to find the guided tour already in progress. It was well worth the effort and we wish we'd made it on time.

The Kansas State Capitol Building had undergone major renovation a few years earlier to the tune of $300 million. The guide explained that centrally located Kansas became the meeting place for many national governmental events, including international affairs.

I used to live across the street from the Utah State Capitol and visited it many times. This Kansas building was far more elaborate and architecturally superior.

The guide pointed out different types of marble used, some from Italy, some from Belgium, etc.

Amelia Earhart and President Eisenhower were from Kansas, so had paintings and statues and such here and there. In 1975 I'd toured Eisenhower's birth home in Abilene. Back then, when you left town, the border of the town was more obvious than I think any other town border I'd ever seen. This big line of trees and houses ended abruptly as the farmland began.

There are tons of wall murals in the Capitol Building. The most famous, a larger than life of John Brown, became an album cover for the band Kansas. We'd missed that part of the tour, but the guide was glad to head back down to that painting and give us the history. It was painted long before any of us were born. At the time, the legislature criticized the painting because it included black slaves, dying civil war soldiers, a tornado and wheat fields on fire. The artist stuck to his guns and the mural painting is now valued even more for those features.

The painter was fired just before he completed the last mural painting. As his last personal commentary on being expelled by people who were not artists and knew nothing about art, he added a family of skunks at the bottom of the unfinished mural, representing his bureaucratic critics.

From the Capitol, we said our good-byes and thank yous and love yous to Aunt Lana to head-up the 168 miles to Lincoln, NE. A bit outside of town is the Pawnee State Park. It's a very lovely park for a camping area. Lots of grass. Nice sized camping sites.

I'd reserved the spot second from the end, closest to Pawnee Lake. What you don't see when reserving such areas is that there's no beach access nearby our camping spot. We would have had to go a mile or so up the road to get to a decent beach. No biggie. Neither of us were planning on swimming or fishing.

Also, payments to stay there are weird. You can pay $25 for an electric site, or $30 for a full amenities site. I paid $30, but there were no full amenities sites. None. I checked. All only had electricity. No water or sewer. They had a water station near the entrance. No dump station I could find on site, even if I paid for them. Second, we also had to pay an extra eight bucks as out-of-staters just to enter the park. Five bucks if you live in state, so double charges. Paying for camping apparently didn't cover the park use fee.

With that said, the amounts were very affordable, and cheaper than most RV parks. Also, this spot seemed much nicer than most RV parks. It had a permanent picnic table and fire pit. We made campfires to sit around and play guitar and eat yummy schtuff. Unfortunately, the mosquitos were so bad, as soon as the dusk started you had to go inside.

Margaret, whom we'd seen at Lana's in Topeka, came to visit with us all three days, the whole time she was off work. It was great getting more acquainted with her.

Amy, Margaret and I took a walk along the lake to see if there was a beach close by. There was not, or at least not one within walking proximity. The park there is beautifully maintained, offering a grassy area along the lake for day use only. We didn't find a swimming/wading beach, but there was lots of firewood to tote back to our camp.

Amy's cousin Stephanie came with her two children, Michael and Ezra. Young Ezra was a handful. He'd take-off for the street, full throttle, without notice. Mom chased after him at a sprint. There was very little traffic, but still always scary to see the little guy head to the street without caution.

We'd brought a bicycle for me and an electric scooter for Amy. Amy took Ezra out on the scooter for a few rounds, then let the older boy Michael ride the scooter. He hurt his toe the first day, wearing flip flops, so brought shoes the second day, and did much better. He had never ridden a bicycle, so it did not come naturally for him to ride the scooter. He figured it out without getting too hurt.

Another pair of Amy's cousins, Cameron and Amber, also came to visit one morning. Cameron is Stephanie's sister. (I don't expect you to keep track of that. It makes my head spin every time Amy explains who's who in her family.) They worked graveyard shift, so came after being up all night just for a couple hours. They had to get home to let the dogs out. We were supposed to see them the next morning and fix them breakfast, but they cancelled, so only the one visit. C'est la vie. Still very nice for me to meet them.

Margaret came in the afternoon with hamburgers and other goodies for dinner, cooked over the fire of course. As the day ended, the fireflies came out, first in the wooded area next to the campsites. We don't have fireflies in Washington. Amy tried to video them, but approaching the woods only brought mosquitos to feast on her. She abandoned that project very quickly.

After everyone left, we both showered. Getting low on water, we'd have to refill the tank before we left – the water near the entrance to the park.

We filled up with diesel in Lincoln for $2.99/gallon. The most we had to pay per gallon the entire trip. We also stopped for groceries at Russ Market and had breakfast at a close by restaurant.

One nice side of being at the Pawnee State Park was that it was west of town, and we would be heading west the next day. Honestly, a slight sadness touched both Amy and I in Lincoln. Up until that part of our COVID Escape Great Adventure, we were still technically not heading towards home. Even heading north from Arkansas did not give us that impression, but Lincoln would be the left turn to head back west and ultimately towards home. There were still many miles and adventures ahead for us, but Lincoln reminded us we were beginning the end of our wonderful trip.

Our last day in Lincoln, Amy and I went shopping with Morris. Busy day, but still nice and even restful. We started Kai's Market, then ate breakfast at Woodee's, then onto Walmart and Dollar Tree. Amy needed a prescription refill. After some calls and jumping through some hoops, she was able to get it transferred from Rite Aid in Sequim to Walgreens in Lincoln. Apparently, Lincoln has no Rite Aid Pharmacies.

Margaret arrived minutes behind us back at the campsite. She brought stuffed mushrooms to add to the hamburger and hot dogs for dinner.

Stephanie and kids got there around 7 p.m. Then, she had to run pick-up her husband and take him home then come back. We never did see him. Cut into our time together of course. Everyone left after 9 as the dusk and mosquitos approached, ignoring our citronella candles.

There was a big downpour overnight. Lasted for hours. We were more than glad we had not slept in a tent.

THURSDAY, JULY 15th

Our folding chairs were all wet from the rain, so I kept them out of their storage bags as I stowed them. Give them time to dry. I considered putting them on the back with the bike and scooter where the air flow would dry them quickly, (if it didn't rain again).

I want to mention that two camps over, the elderly couple had put-up a dozen flags around the perimeter of their campsite. I'm talking about larger flags, not little one's with a stick you can stick into the ground. They put up a line to hang the flags. They really went to a lot of trouble to make the display. I should've taken a picture. They also had two dogs, so we got to chat about their babies one time when they walked by. Like I said earlier, people we'd never met were often happy to stop and chat at length. I'm sure some sociologists have already done a granted study why this is so.

I-80, the longest road in America. We'd be traversing only a small stretch today, crossing Nebraska.

We refilled the water at Pawnee State Park before heading out. Destination: Julesburg, CO, in the northeasternmost corner of the state, parked right up against the crux of the Nebraska panhandle. They say in Julesburg if you go one mile north, you're in Nebraska, and if you go one mile east, you're in Nebraska. This is where Amy grew up and where her mum presently lived.

After we got Amy's prescription at Walgreens, we headed west. We found an RV dump at a gas station, but the black water tank was clogged. We added more enzyme and water and drove to shake things up. Next time we stopped at a kind of nasty RV dump, everything flowed easily. Whew!

I loved seeing a large, white cross near the Calvary Bible Camp, clearly seen from the interstate.

In our big box, it can be a bit unnerving when the bigger semis pass. Sometimes you think you could roll down your window and touch the aluminum coated box next to you. I was in the right lane, but one semi decided to pace me for miles, side-by-side. That had to piss-off any drivers behind us. I don't think he was being rude or mad at me about something. If anything, he was mad at someone behind us and blocking their way for a bunch of miles. Either way, it was weird having the big semi box beside me mile after mile.

In 2004, I visited family in Delaware. I decided to take a forty-eight-hour trek around New England. Being October, I'd hoped to see some striking fall colors.

Driving along I-95 at night, somewhere in Rhode Island, a pickup truck intentionally came alongside me to block the car behind it. Suddenly, I was thrust into a confrontation I wanted no part of. I tried speeding up. The pickup kept pace. I slowed way down. Same response. So, I just rode it out with a slower speed and after some miles as we approached Providence, the truck put on the gas and went ahead of me.

It's always odd when you're in those moments and you don't know if you'll become the target of some stranger's anger, thereby uncertain what they might do. Would I turn into a stunt driver in the moment, driving crazily, even flipping around to drive the wrong direction on the freeway? There were no other cars out that night. Perhaps I'd run into them with the rented car to push them off the road while I made my escape?

James Bond would have loved what I imagined in that moment.

Back on I-80 that afternoon, I just had to keep pace and let the miles become my advocates. I thought he'd pass, but on some little hill I went on ahead. I loved my Cummins diesel, but when I reached cruising speed, it would not go any faster. That's just how fast it would be willing to go.

This was Amy's home turf. She spent a bunch of her formative years in this neighborhood of the nation. Her dad was a wheat farmer, so she learned the ways of working the earth. She learned to drive on the farm in an old pickup with a manual transmission. She had countless little stories to share as we got closer to Julesburg.

Amy's mum has a place that was meant to be at least a duplex. She never rented out the other half, thereby never making the money she expected from the dwelling. When I first went there, she was living in the lower lever. Rather cave like. This time, she'd moved to the upper floor. More open with a few windows. She slept in the smaller bedroom near the living room and kitchen so she wouldn't have to move as far. Amy and I stayed in the master bedroom with its own bathroom.

Leaving Central Time Zone for Mountain, we gained the hour, arriving in Julesburg around 4 p.m., MDT. We'd planned this to be our longest stay of our COVID Escape Tour.

Amy's mum, named Jackie, spends most of her days in her easy chair watching old western TV programs. Gunsmoke is her favorite, but she also likes Cheyenne and The Rifleman. I'm sure she has a thing for James Arness, or Clint Walker, or Chuck Connor (or all 3). She has an elderly man named Doug who does much of her building maintenance. He was building new steps outside the back door. Amy has known him her entire life.

Amy and I took her car to the grocery store for some food. She doesn't get out often and needed much. I had already gotten a thirty amp plug from Home Depot, so physically replaced the RV plug. It worked fine, then I used the adapter for common house current. We parked on the lawn, then hooked up to an extension cord coming out her front door.

We all got cleaned up and went to dinner at the one café in town, called D&J, or the locals call it Joe's. It totally fits the image of a greasy spoon, small town eatery. Perfect place to go for dinner. Verily, I loved seeing the town, the people, and their lives. Farming is King there. I didn't grow up there, so enjoyed the newness of it all.

Awakening the next day on a too soft bed, we again went to D&J's for breakfast. Nowhere else in town to go.

Amy's big brother Jim still owns and works the family farm. He had a managerial job in Illinois for oil production. When President Biden shut down the Canada pipeline, Jim lost his position and had to be reassigned. He still had his home in Julesburg, though much of the farm is in Nebraska. His wife Jenny stayed in the house, hung-out with their grandkids and oversaw some matters of the farm. She also helped take care of her very aged dad who also lived in Julesburg. We visited at their home for a bit. I toured some of the property, seeing what had changed since my last visit. They no longer had cattle.

They'd arranged for all to meet for lunch in Chappell, NE at The Rusty Bucket. Jim's son John, wife Amanda and their family joined us. Also, Amy's stepmother Kathy and her friend Penny came - the only time we'd see them. We'd last seen Kathy at Grandma Emily's 100th birthday.

Life can be Very Funny. Amy who grew up on a wheat farm is now gluten free. Not a lot of specifically gluten free options offered there in the Wheat Belt eateries.

After lunch, we went to the farm. Jim came home from Illinois because it was wheat harvest. When the wheat is ready to be harvested, the farmer has just a few days to get it mowed before it's past its expiration date and unsellable. Jim and his son John were adjusting the Combine when we got there. Amy asked if I could take a ride with Jim in the combine. I got quite the thrill to watch him harvest over thirty-five acres. We talked about harvesting as well as politics, God and who knows what else.

As we finished up, I said to Jim, "It's a lot like mowing the lawn."

It took better part of two hours to finish that part of the harvest. Amy and John drove a truck, keeping pace with the combine, towing a trailer which would receive the mowed grain so Jim could keep mowing.

When Grandma Emily passed away, the farm was divided between Lana and Amy's dad. Since her dad was already deceased, that half of the farm went to the four kids. Amy got a share of the harvest and learned about selling wheat. She has downloaded an app on her phone so she can check prices daily in real time. When it went near six and a quarter a bushel, she sold. Jim had told her anything over six was a pretty good price, and this year was one of the best harvests he'd ever seen. Amy and siblings received nothing from the harvest last year. So, we got a few welcomed bucks to help pay for our COVID Escape excursion.

Amy's mum had come to the farm as well. She could not be out in the fields, so napped in her car for spell, then Jenny took her home. We had no idea we would be out on the wheat fields so long when we left to ride the combine.

When we got home, we got some weed poison to spray part of mom's yard. Not much evidence it was doing anything before we left. We were told some days later that yes, the weeds were dying and a bit of grass growing in its place.

Amy wanted me to see the train depot which had long ago been made into a museum. It was closed and gutted and being rebuilt. She went in and chatted with a worker who said it wouldn't be done till around October.

We fixed nachos for dinner at Jackie's home, and chatted alongside the black and white westerns until around ten when Jackie went to bed. I went out to our RV to play guitar until around midnight.

FRIDAY, JULY 16th

This would be a very special day. Skydiving. Neither of us had ever been skydiving before. I chickened out jumping out of the airplane, so settled for wing-walking.

Then, we went white-water rafting on the Platte River. We fished the river between the rapids and caught enough trout for a fine dinner.

Finally, we cooked our trout over open coals, drank some fine wine Amy brought last minute, and sang show tunes under the stars. No mosquitoes bugged us the entire evening.

Actually, none of that happened. As I edited this book, I realized I missed a day, but for the life of me, I cannot recall what we did. So, skydiving, white-water rafting, fishing, eating, singing will be the official report for this day. By this time of summer, the North Platte River ain't got enough water to take any inflatable raft downstream, much less call it white water rapids.

SATURDAY, July 17th

Jackie expected to go out to D&J's restaurant to buy us breakfast again. I said that was silly, so fixed eggs, bacon and toast. The rest of the day, Amy and I cleaned Jackie's house. When we later went to the store, I'd seen a large outside wall mural paying homage to the Denver Broncos. Well, we were in Colorado. I was wearing a Seattle Seahawks shirt and had Amy take my picture in front of the wall.

Dave Outside Denver Bronco's Wall, Julesburg, CO

We'd already made arrangements with Pastor Alan (Amy's cousin) and his wife Sylvia to attend a graduation party for a woman named Marilyn. She had four boys all graduating from something, and threw the big bash in a hall by the firehouse. Good food and company, (mostly Mexican). Most of the time we visited with Alan and Sylvia - our first chance to do so since we'd arrived. We talked about Jackie and her not attending church. He would do more to encourage her to come and help her any other way he could.

Amy also got to see a woman with whom she'd gone to grade school. Amy recognized her first. Another fun surprise for our trip.

Returning in time to see Amy's mum for a bit, then she went off to bed. Amy and I went out to Morris to practice songs to play at Alan's church tomorrow morning, plus just had a wonderful praise and worship time together.

SUNDAY, July 18th

This was to be the day we were to leave, originally. We would attend Alan's service, have lunch and head north to Mount Rushmore. Rushmore got taken off the map for a spell, then added, then removed. Our time limitation always looked forward to the Stoeckl Family Reunion in Florence, Oregon to be held July 25th through the 28th. One week away. So, Rushmore kept getting axed as our plans and visits adjusted for our hosts. I'd never been to Rushmore, so really wanted to go. Amy grew up fairly close to Rushmore, so had seen it often.

Alan's church is right across the street from Jackie's house. Literally across the street. We walked over to practice with the worship team before the service. They have a piano player who uses real music without guitar chords, so I sat out playing with the choir. Amy would sing with them – an added blessing since one of their members would be gone that day. Their ensemble included the pianist, four singers and sometimes a guitar player. Pastor Alan sometimes played his trombone behind the singers.

After the main worship, Amy and I sang two songs for the congregation. It was clear most of them had never heard either song – *John 3:16* and *It Is Well* – the *Bethel Church* version. Both were still very well received.

Pastor Alan gave his sermon, one more song, and we retired to the social area for a potluck meal. Since COVID, such shared meals had been taboo – an odd requirement since COVID isn't shared by eating something. Our stomach acids kill COVID just peachy.

It's passed by air into our lungs and becomes its obnoxious presence.

Jenny's dad attended that church. He sat alone eating. Amy went over to say hi. He'd not realized earlier who she was. I had a long chat with a woman named Kim, and another native American who was covered with tattoos and wore a feather. Both were great to get acquainted with.

Back at Jackie's, she had a double-layer, queen sized, foam rubber mattress pad downstairs in the unused apartment. Our mattress liked to irritate my lower back at times, so we accepted Jackie's gift and placed it in Morris. Actually, it was a good choice for my back didn't hurt much after we started sleeping on the extra layers. Only the fitted sheet objected to having to stretch so tight. (*Wah!*)

Later, we piled into Jackie's car to drive to Sidney, NE for dinner with Jim, Jenny and others. Sidney has the distinction of having the first Cabela's Store. We were blocks away from Cabela's, dining just off the freeway at a Mexican restaurant called Margarita's.

In the restaurant, Amy and I sat by John and Amanda's three kids. The younger girl looked fine while we were there, but developed appendicitis a couple days after we left and had to have emergency surgery. Jim later reported other problems after eating at Margarita's, so it's off their list.

Driving back to Julesburg, I remarked how straight the road, and how smoothly Jackie's car drove, even at eighty.

MONDAY, JULY 19th

As I'd recently mentioned, Mount Rushmore had been on and off the table throughout our travels. One of Amy's cousins, Robin, who lives near Nampa, ID, cancelled having us come. That freed-up two days to do whatever, and guess what got re-added to our itinerary? Yup. Mount Rushmore.

Heading into Nebraska, we passed through Osh Kosh, where Grandma Emily used to live. No reason to drive through or reminisce.

Before Scotts Bluff, Amy and I stopped at Chimney Rock. There's another Chimney Rock in North Carolina if you do a Google search. This one is off Highway 92 in Nebraska. Amy had been there often. I'd never seen or heard of it. Not super big, but still kind of cool to see.

They had a Visitor's Center that cost $8 to enter. We paid. Not worth the money. It's a nice building, but the exhibits are pretty bleak, and you don't get that close to Chimney Rock.

We continued towards Scott's Bluff to have lunch with another one of Amy's cousins, named Rhea. She came with her granddaughter. We met at Culver's. They offered salads. I got a burger and fries. All very good food. Rhea owned a used bookstore, so they chatted about that as well as getting Rhea caught-up on Jackie's health concerns.

I tried to fill-up with diesel at a Maverik station. The pump wouldn't work, so I left a bit miffed, forgetting to replace the fuel cap for the second time this trip. Another ten bucks I didn't need to throw away.

Zipping north, we got to Mount Rushmore around 6 p.m. Lots of daylight left for this exhibit. Morris didn't like the last hill and threatened to overheat, but as we crested, it settled down and did fine. That was the most concerned I'd been about Morris getting too hot and boiling over. I still suspect the temperature gage is not completely accurate.

You get a sweet look at the Presidentially carved mountain before you even park. Being an RV, we had to park in a special lot. Lots of people out there, wearing masks, directing traffic and telling us where to go. We parked, had a quick bite to eat, then headed in. Past the entrance, some stores and an ice cream stand, you enter a row of state flags, complete with a state name plate at the base, all leading the way to the mountain.

Mount Rushmore has to be one of the most patriotic places I've ever seen. Even Washington D.C. and Boston were not as patriotic. They have some exhibits along the way to check out. We took the Presidential Walk which takes you right to the base of the mountain. I would have loved to climb upward, but knew that would not be allowed and I'm too old to get up the mountain very far without being apprehended and brought back down. Maybe when I was younger????????

Hanging out at one of the view terraces beneath Lincoln, we got chatting with a man from West Virginia.

After the hike, we checked out a few of the exhibits and movies in the Visitors Center. There's a very large outdoor theater which offers a light show and movie about the making of Rushmore. That was actually amazing to see, how they drilled many holes in the surface, placed dynamite and blasted off the rock to the perfect depth, over and over. Some scaling, of course, but it was impressive how cleanly the workers, hanging by ropes over the side of the mountain, worked to build each president.

I'd also never noticed that George Washington's coat continues down the mountain a ways. Thereby, his is the largest of the sculpted Presidents.

Mount Rushmore at Night

During the outdoor presentation at dusk, we enjoyed the movie. They lit up the presidents, bright lights shining upward from just above our position. They invited everyone who was a veteran or active military on the large stage. I estimate over one-hundred people, mostly men, went on stage, including myself.

I urged Amy to come down with me. She was never officially in the US military, but she was married to a sailor for 21 years. She lived the US military life, moving from base to base and taking care of family while her first husband spent many weeks each year at sea.

The ranger picked six randomly and had them take down the US flag. It was fun to watch. They folded it the long way just fine, but when they started the triangular folds, other veterans standing close-by quickly objected. They were folding it backwards. The stars and blue are to be displayed on top.

Leaving Mount Rushmore, we knew it'd be a long drive to North Ogden and Rick and Cindy's the next day. Amy suggested we skedaddle and make some of the miles to Ogden that night. I'd fixed the headlight problem we'd encountered at North Rim and am always game for a night drive. I'm a driveaholic. You don't have to twist my arm very hard to get me to want to drive, so we actually escaped the traffic of Rushmore pretty quickly and headed towards Newcastle, WY.

There is so much to see around Mount Rushmore. Some people after that said, "Did you see this or that?" Nope. No time. We had to get to the family reunion and had a lot of miles to cover before we could get there. We also had timely reservations to see the redwood forests near Crescent City, CA. Amy had never been through the redwoods before. That was her "Rushmore", along with the Grand Canyon.

I knew we were passing through some beautiful country that we could barely see at night. We got to Newcastle. I didn't really see anywhere good to stop, so kept going. Leaving Highway 85 for dinky Highway 450, we drove through miles and miles of open darkness to Wright, WY. I kept close watch on the road for wildlife. Remarkably, only three vehicles passed us the entire seventy-two miles to Wright. We found a very small truck stop, so parked amongst the semis. The one next to us had its engine running. I was surprised that they kept the engine running literally all night. I expected it to be turned-off any minute after we arrived. For Amy, it was difficult to sleep with the never-ending grumbling. For me, it was better than having a white noise fan blowing in the room.

Now, I'd never been to Wright, WY before that day. For that matter, I probably saw it on a map some past decade, but found no reason to have given it any notice. Nowadays I would have noticed a bit more. My second child married a man named Wright, so I would have had that name association. Still, I wasn't expecting much and would not have been surprised to have to continue to Casper, but I'll tell you, I don't know what's going on there, but it's something big. There were tons of big industrial things going on. I'm expecting all federal government. I would not have been surprised to learn they have nuclear missile silos there or its own Area 51 or something. Lots of activity for a dinky, very remote town.

TUESDAY, JULY 20th

Leaving Wright, we made it to Casper and found a fuel cap at Napa Auto Parts. They even let me take the cap out to test it, then come back in and pay for it. We found a Starbucks and treated ourselves to coffee and breakfast.

We'd bought a Keurig style coffee maker at Walmart for $20 before we left. It's perfect for the RV. You add the cup of water and your K-cup, press the button and wait. It takes a little longer for each cup than a conventional Keurig because it only heats one cup of water at a time, but when you're done, you unplug it and put it back in the cupboard. No water left to spill out. It's been one of our better purchases.

Continuing down the road, we refilled the tank at Rock Springs, WY on I-80. Crossing the street from the gas station, we ate at the Southwest Grill. Yum! Steak and fries with green chili salsa and Navaho tacos. I'd been wanting Navaho tacos since we'd been in Arizona. We stopped at a couple more rest stops along the way. In Utah, near Echo, there are dozens of prairie dog holes in this one section that you walk past to see the mountains and take pictures.

We got to Rick and Cindy's around 6:30. They took us out for ice cream which we didn't finish and meant to take with us the next day and, of course, forgot. We'd left gallon bottles of frozen water in their freezer our first visit. Apparently, none of us learned the first time.

It was good to get cleaned up. Early to bed.

WEDNESDAY, JULY 21st.

Leaving Rick and Cindy's around 8:30 a.m., we drove to Riverdale, south side of Ogden, to have our oil changed and the chassis lubed. There was a Del Taco close by. Apparently, we'd not had enough Mexican food this trip.

The Salt Flats were as plain as I'd ever seen them. Living in Ogden and Salt Lake, we would occasionally visit Wendover on the Utah/Nevada border. You can readily deduce where the border is placed. Wendover's a sorry looking little town on the Utah side. Cross the border, and big casinos rule. I'd go for a weekend with my first wife, Ann, or take one-day road trips with Rob just to get out of town.

Many years back, I drove across the Salt Flats with the setting sun directly ahead for most of the drive to Wendover. I mean, the sun stood upon I-80 right in front of me for a chunk of the drive. Very obnoxious. I felt glad I'd bought new sunglasses in Salt Lake before we headed west, not that they would block that much sunlight. After we got to Wendover, the interstate turns off from heading directly into the sun.

Back to our 2021 trip, the cooler weather we'd been blessed with earlier in our travels had given way to the real summer. It was a hot, 100° plus drive across western Utah and Nevada. The AC did a good job, but it was still hot. Lots of fires in Oregon and points north made the air hazy, and I'm sure Greenhouse Effect hotter. We made reservations in Winnemucca, NV at Silver State RV Park. After the pool, I took a shower and when I returned to Morris, Amy had hung some LED tape lighting around the cabin. Very fun and romantic!

147

Pastor Alan commonly does online sermons, practically every morning. We watched one of his sermons from that morning while listening to strong wind gusts outside the RV. A couple from Tacoma arrived around midnight. We chatted about Washington the next morning. Like us, they would also be heading north out of Winnemucca. I'm pretty sure we passed them later as they stopped at an overlook.

THURSDAY, JULY 22ⁿᵈ

We drove north on Highway 95, from Winnemucca to Klamath Falls, OR. A lot more mountains and windy roads than I-80 from Salt Lake to Winnemucca. Highway 95 brings you to Highway 140 – a very remote, 2-lane stretch of road. No cell signal for about 2 hours. It's not particularly scenic, but somehow still a very sweet stretch of road to drive.

I'll jump ahead here to mention that Rick and Cindy took the same road to the family reunion two days after us. We talked about our drive and Rick was amazed I'd made it in Morris going that direction.

Somehow the terrible smoke from the Oregon forest fires became little to none outside Winnemucca. Even Klamath Falls had little smoke pollution – an interesting mystery since along the highway we even drove past a firefighter's camp.

The main road out of Winnemucca is pretty straight and worn out. Then, you enter the mountain regions, going up and down and up again. Some nice twists near cliffs with a great view. Unfortunately, it was the one time it made Amy a bit carsick. She had been so pleased. Prone to carsickness in cars, she had been thrilled to not encounter the nausea in Morris. She could even look at her phone while I drove – a common BIG trigger for her carsickness. This road wound no more than other roads we'd been on around Rushmore and over many mountain passes, but this time it irritated her stomach.

We stayed at the Klamath KOA. It's obnoxious to get to from the southeast. The GPS takes you right through the city and along roads that were not meant to be driven by bigger vehicles. We did fine, of course, but seems like there should have been a better way to get us there. As you know, GPS does not ask what kind of vehicle you are driving.

This KOA had a nice swimming pool. We met a couple named Dean and Debbie, traveling with their grandson Lincoln. They loved our old Allegro. They had a much newer rig, but said they'd had the same Allegro some years back and loved it.

The on/off switch for the generator, inside on the dashboard, stopped working. It has an on/off switch by the generator. The dash switch would still start the generator, but not turn it off, so I pulled off the toggle and tried to see if I could clean the contacts enough for it to stop. Nope. Still not working. I'll have to fix it when we get home.

I cooked butter chicken curry for dinner. We discovered we did not have any cooking oil, so I cooked some bacon and used that fat for the butter chicken. Everything tastes better with bacon. Then, we sat outside while I played guitar for a bit before bed. Lots of people out all evening at that RV park. Some RV parks have more long-term tenants. They're not on vacation, so you never see them. This was definitely a vacation crowd, all enjoying the evening cool outside.

For me, I was more tired today, so we retired early.

FRIDAY, JULY 23rd

Klamath Falls to Crescent City, CA. Nothing notable before we left Klamath RV park. Today would be a shorter drive than the previous two days from North Ogden. Lots of beauty to behold during this drive including Klamath Lake and the mountains south of Medford, OR. We took I-5 from Medford to Grants Pass.

My brother John and his wife Andie live in Grants Pass, so we got together with them for lunch.

Just arranging to meet John and Andie was a silly adventure. They were preparing for the family reunion, starting in two days, so said their home was a wreck. They had us meet them in the Fred Meyer parking lot, then when we met up, they had to get gas. Amy and I left Morris there to ride with J&A.

We dined at the Taprock Northwest Grill. It overlooks the Rogue River. They offered outdoor seating, but Andie preferred to remain indoors, and we sat by the window with a river view. Tour boats went up and down the river during our brief dining experience. John and Andie had taken the boats for a fun excursion over the last year or two. If we'd had time... We did our customary pics outside the restaurant, then headed on our way.

Crescent City, CA is on the Pacific coast, so from Grants Pass, best to take Highway 199. It gets very windy, (not as in lots of wind, but as in lots of curves and turns,) having been built around the huge redwood trees. I wondered if they had to take any trees out while they were building it? At first, I thought an absolute yes, but roads and trails would have been well established through the passes well before the highway was paved.

If they did have to remove any of these old, majestic trees, I expect it was not that many.

We stayed at the Crescent Village Camper Inn RV Park. That's a mouthful. Ron is one of the proprietors. He led us, driving his golf cart, to our RV space. He was a hoot and explained that this was his wife's park. Not his. He just did whatever she wanted him to do.

The space was tight to maneuver Morris into, backing in. Basically, the paved road is not that wide, being one way, so single lane. Worse, the grass across from our RV space suddenly slopes down deeply a few feet. No way I could drive Morris on it. We'd high center for sure. So, it took at least a few tries to get Morris backed in properly.

After we were settled, I really wanted to go see the Pacific Ocean. We should've taken our bike and scooter, but I love walking and hiking, so lured Amy into what turned out to be a four mile walk to the Pacific Ocean. On the bright side, it was not too hot and slightly breezy. It was also nice to just explore that part of the town.

We like Necco Wafers and found some at a CVS Pharmacy. They were cheaper if I got their ID card. The closest CVS to Sequim is Poulsbo, almost an hour away. We don't go by there that often.

Reaching the ocean, it offered an overlook. The beach lay far below. We could've found a trail to go down, but after our little hike, we were content to sit on the bench and enjoy the pre-sunset. They had one section with an intended viewpoint a little south of our position. It had informational postings, so we walked down, read the metal words, and decided to call a taxi to return to the RV park. Our taxi driver was named

Cora. She was also a hoot, and we scheduled with her to come get us the next morning at 10:30.

After the walk, I decided it was time to get the bike out and ride it around the RV park. I think part of me was saying, "You brought this along. You're almost done with your Grand Adventure and haven't ridden it once.

Grants Pass leftovers for dinner, played cribbage and slept well.

SATURDAY, JULY 24th

10:30 appointment with Cora's taxi took us to Avis at the small airport. We'd called ahead to make sure they had a car. When we got there, the guy wanted to charge us $83 to have the car for just a few hours. Not even a full day! We wisely decided against it. Fortunately, Cora was still there when we left Avis. It was too far to walk back to town, or at least farther than most people would care to walk.

Cora took us to Coast Auto Sales, a used car dealership in town that rented cars. We'd already called them the day before, so were not surprised when she came out and said they were under new management and still making adjustments in their business, so did not yet have any cars to rent. In short, Amy and I spent $37 without getting a rental car to explore the Redwoods without Morris.

Cora suggested the best way to explore the Redwoods was to drive up a dirt road west of town that would take us to Stout Grove. She gave directions. I asked if we could take a big motorhome and she said it would not be a problem. She was mistaken. With that said, we still made it in Morris, but I would not recommend it.

Stopping at Walmart for a few items we probably did not really need other than ice, we easily found the dirt road. It's a single lane with wide spots for vehicles to pass, nine miles long. In Morris, we went even slower than most, but no worries. We were in no hurry.

At one point, a pickup truck, passing us, going the other direction, stopped to say we were not going make it. He did not elaborate, but we soon discovered what

154

he meant. A couple/three hundred yards later we came to a tight squeeze between three trees, angle left, angle right, angle left and hope you don't hit the first tree. One of those kind of places. Morris is eight feet wide, plus mirrors. Somehow I maneuvered him through, the mirrors barely inches from the trees, but nothing scraped. There were lots of similar tight squeezes, but that one was the tightest.

And what would we have done if we couldn't make it? It was not like we could just turn around and go back down. Not at all. I saw absolutely nowhere along the way that was wide enough for a 31' motor home to turn around. Thank You Jesus. We made it slowly but just fine. And, honestly, if it had room for our mirror extended, it had adequate room for us to get through.

About six miles in, you come to a turn-off to the Stout Grove. Most people, including myself, expected the trees to be bigger around, but it's named Stout for Mr. Stout who used to live there. It has a mile long hiking trail that circles through the trees. Part of it overlooks the Smith River, named for Jedediah Smith, an early explorer and settler. That part of the National Park is also named after him.

We found a more than adequately wide place to park Morris to take the well shaded hike. There are not a lot of signs. Amy and others went off trail. When you're walking, you've been in sight of the Smith River for some time, so the trail seems to keep following the river. If you go that way, the trail gets narrower and narrower. I expect it never ends and brings you out at the road before the bridge near Highway 199. After we'd gone not quite a mile off the circle, I told Amy we were off trail, so we turned back. We shared that info with other hikers who also turned back. When we got back to the trail, it was obvious which way to go to continue the circle.

Amy in the Redwood Forest, California

Back in Morris, a few more miles and you're back on Highway 199. I wouldn't advise anyone to take their motor home on that road – even less if you're towing a trailer, but it is navigable. Just a few miles west along Highway 199, we came to the Jedediah Smith Visitor Center. We stopped in, used the bathrooms, toured the displays and had lunch in Morris in the parking lot. Amy found a nice Redwoods jacket for a decent price. Not the usual price gouging we would have expected.

Continuing along the highway, we came upon Walker Lane. You drive through more narrow passages between trees to come riverside. Not as bad as the Stout Grove drive, but on the other hand... well, you'll see. We parked on the sand and dirt above the river. A couple families were there enjoying the water. We met a couple came named Dave and Kim, from Bodfish, CA, near Bakersfield. We walked down to the water, skipped a few rocks, then had to figure out how to get Morris turned around. The road sloped down to the water with sand I expect would have gotten Morris stuck. There was a less used trail to our right, so I took that. In hindsight, I should have walked it first to see what we would find. It took us back to the beach, but I could turn onto something of a dirt road that would bring us back to the main way to exit. Dave and Kim helped guide me. Like most motorhomes, Morris doesn't turn on a dime, so got a bit side tilted as I completed the tight turn. I gave it the gas to create momentum to get past the softer sandy bit of road without incidence.

It's fun how life inadvertently prepares a person for something they would encounter years later. When I was a kid in Ogden, we had lots of fields right by my house. All of us boys bought cheap cars to drive in the fields. You could get a decent clunker for less than a hundred bucks in those days. Some of those cars became licensed and street legal, but not all. We became very adept at driving on dirt roads.

Next, I worked for Blaine Public Works for five years, in Blaine, WA, right on the US/Canada border. I drove some crazy trucks and tractors on tilted slopes that felt like you might flip over and roll. Such casualties never happened, but it helped to prepare me for driving Morris on a sloped dirt road with confidence it would not be top heavy and flip over.

Heading back to Crescent City, we explored the town, driving along the parks and coastal areas for a bit. We saw a Dollar Tree store so picked up a few things, then heading back to the RV park. The backing in went a little easier this time, but not much. We had dinner, played some more cribbage and talked about plans for the upcoming year.

Finally, after we arrived back at the RV park, we encountered an miracle. Not a HUGE miracle, but a miracle all the same.

As I mentioned, we'd dined in Morris at the Jedediah Smith Visitor Center parking lot. We both poured drinks in plastic cups for our meal. Fruit juice, I think. When we finished, for no reason I can imagine, we left both cups on the dining table.

The dining table is just a hardtop, Formica type of table. We are completely and utterly awed to find, after driving windy Highway 199, then maneuvering Morris through the Walker Lane trails, then exploring Crescent City beaches to finally back into the RV parking space, neither cup of juice had spilled, or even moved. There's no way without divine intervention that either of those cups should have made the final journey. Sometimes God gives us these very small but clearly observable miracles to say, "Hi. I'm still here and I've got your back." I love those moments and praise Him mightily. It's not like we could not have cleaned up a little spilled juice, but the fact neither glass moved cannot be within the real and clear laws of physics on this planet.

As I like to say, "Divine coincidence is never a coincidence."

SUNDAY, JULY 25th
Family Reunion near Florence, OR

Hard rain and wind came overnight to blow us out of town. Taking Highway 101 northbound, I said a very sobering thing to Amy. You know, if we stayed on this road, it would totally take us home. Sequim is parked up against Highway 101 on the Olympic Peninsula. We could have stayed on 101 all the way to our off ramp. Another sad indicator our Grand Adventure was nearing its end.

It would not be many miles before we were back in Oregon. Still, before we left California, we drove past a man on foot on 101 holding a gun in his right hand, pointed in the general direction of the passing cars. There was another man walking say two-hundred yards further. I saw nothing in our brief drive past to say those two were related, but part of the overall observation at that moment.

When you see someone holding a gun in their hand, standing on a busy highway, it gets your attention. If he'd had it holstered, no biggie, but out in his hand, I would not care to guess his intentions. We called 911. She'd already received other calls, and said right up front, "Is this about the man with the gun on 101?"

I took notice of the businesses close-by to give location. The dispatcher made sure whether it was the California or Oregon side. We gave her a lot of details of where we saw the man as well as description of what he was wearing. Of course, we continued up the road and have no idea what came of the contact and when the Highway Patrol or Sheriff contacted the man.

Being Sunday, I kept eyes open for a church to attend. We attend a Nazarene Church in Carlsborg, WA, next to Sequim. While passing through Brookings, OR, I saw a Nazarene Church, about ready to start the service. I hit the brakes hard to make the next turn, enjoyed seeing a little bit of a Brookings neighborhood as I sought a place to turn around, and joined in with the church service. Amy shared a little less enthusiasm of my driving skills and prowess at that moment.

After church, we got to chat with Pastor Mike. I expect such churches have regular visitors most weeks – people who love the LORD, but will never be back. I pay tithe regularly. For this trip, I gave a little to each church each week. That made more sense than giving my entire monthly tithe to any one church we visited.

At Carlsborg Family Church, we've been trying to set up live streaming for quite some time. After the service, I introduced myself to a man named Rick running the sound booth. He was very helpful to share how they put together their production each week. I took pictures to help me remember better after we left.

We stopped at Wendy's in Coos Bay, OR. The inside was open for people to sit. One couple next to us were looking at their iPad, watching a friend from Coos Bay who was competing in the Olympics. How exciting. I'm sorry I did not write down the athlete's name.

The Oregon Coast really is a beautiful drive. It got very windy in places, trying to toss around our big box. Florence is halfway up the state, so lots of miles to enjoy the scenery.

My dad and mum had moved to Florence in the early 1990's. Living in Ogden when dad retired from civil service for the US government, working at Hill Air

Force Base his last stint, neither of them had ever been to *The Beautiful Oregon Coast.* They took a little vacation and loved it. They went back a few months later, and decided to move there. A couple/three more trips and they decided on Florence. They sold the house in Ogden and bought a nice little three-bedroom place in the heart of Florence.

My family has reunions every two years – typically, starting in 1994. COVID canceled the 2020 reunion. These get-togethers are always camping trips, and for the first bunch, were always held in a different campsite. My dad passed away in 1999, but my mum, now 85, lives south of Portland with my sister Jeanne and husband Bill. To accommodate her, we seek places closer to her home. This time, they did not rent an RV, but got a motel in town.

We met at the Sutton Campground. We'd been there for 2004 reunion. This would be the first time we returned to a previous family reunion location. My brother Jay and Jennifer married there in Florence after the reunion. This reunion had been arranged as a memorial for my nephew Kevin who at 28, died the previous year from a lengthy battle with colon cancer. Kevin was John's son, (whom we'd visited in Grants Pass three days back.)

Around thirty of us came from the Stoeckl clan. I mentioned my mum, the matriarch, who came with Bill and Jeanne. All six of my brothers and sisters came. Some of the kids and grandkids came. I'm the oldest of the seven.

Being Kevin's memorial, we also had some of the Hiss family there. My Aunt Jeanne is mum's younger sister who married Roger Hiss way back when. Uncle

Roger passed away years back, but Jeanne and three of her kids joined us. It's ALWAYS such a delight to see them. The years of distance are always villains to overcome.

Mum's older brother, my Uncle Ray came, who lives near Seattle. He brought his dog, Lady. Divorced for quite some years, he always, always had a dog to share his home. Even at this elderly age, when his last dog died, he promptly got Lady.

There are a few classic themes or activities to all of our reunions. First, most of us kids play guitar, so lots and lots of music around the campfire, especially in the evenings.

Second, good food, of course. We drink alcohol, but to date no one gets totally wasted, and no one has ever been drunkenly obnoxious. For that matter, that also goes for when we've gotten together during visits, in homes, or wherever. It's a very appreciated facet of my family.

Before the reunion, groups are arranged to make dinner. Breakfast and lunch, you're on your own most reunions, but dinners are made by an arranged group for the entire family. The first night we had pasta and salad. Unfortunately, Amy is gluten free, and could not eat the dinner. It was something John and Andie knew who were part of that evening's dinner since it came up years earlier when we all got together for dinner at Uncle Ray's and they fixed spaghetti. Inconsideration? Maybe? Probably? Sometimes families can be so fickle, can't they?

Third, horseshoes. I don't think we've had a reunion without horseshoes to throw.

With the COVID crap, some kept their distance. No one wore a mask throughout the day, but some avoided hugs. That's fine, but none of the hug avoiders avoided sitting shoulder to shoulder around the fire in the evening. C'est la vie! Such consistency is seldom a human trait where families are involved.

Seeing Paul, Alicia and the grandkids from Ellensburg, WA, our first stop of the Grand Tour, on June 18th, Paul admitted to me when they'd took a ride in Morris, he was sure we would not make the whole vacation without a breakdown along the way. He intentionally held his tongue at the time, and now that we'd made it most of the way, he could share his concern and appreciation that we'd made it that far without incidence. Fun!

This evening as the guitars came out, I decided to hang back and let the others play. I'd decided to not bring out my guitar at all that evening. Nobody seemed to care or notice, which was fine, and I totally enjoyed the rich gifts of voices and instruments sharing their talents. Most notably, my niece Rita and her guy Ed play in a semi-country band, singing a bunch of old songs. It was sweet to hear them share their talents.

We were one of the few with a motorhome. My brother Jay with whom we'd spent three days with back in June, set up his parking camp, and selected a good place for our motorhome to park. It was a little away from the others which was more than fine. Jay's wife Jenn could not come because of care for their dogs, but Jay did bring Jagon, the puppy we'd seen in June who, of course, had grown a bunch. He was still happy, happy, happy to see everyone. We wound up spending much of the reunion chatting and sharing time with Jay who's become my closest brother in recent years.

Jay and John are twins, ten years younger than moi. They'd had a bit of a falling out in the previous year or two and could mend quite a bit at this get-together.

MONDAY, JULY 26th

Jay knocked on our door to get our day started. He brought oatmeal and peaches. We dined and chatted and visited till almost noon.

Today would be Kevin's memorial. We went to Devil's Elbow, south of Florence, for the casual service. My dad's ashes were spread there in 1999, and since then, my family calls it Angel's Elbow, or just the Elbow.

Andie had made an extraordinary picture, about 2'X3', of Kevin. One of those pictures made of tiny pictures. After the reunion, she emailed the file to everyone. My son Paul, the pastor, officiated the service. We all got a chance to share a Kevin story or two. Unfortunately, Kevin's wife Meghan could not attend.

It was cloudy and cold and foggy, so we huddled together. There's a little creek there that flows into the Pacific. We could not spread his ashes, but they'd brought slips of paper for everyone to write a prayer, a good-bye or whatever to Kevin. The papers were all burned up and the ashes added to rose petals. We all stood by the creek, grabbed a handful of petals and spread them for our private good-bye to a wonderful young man who'd left us far too early.

I shared a story about when we'd gone to visit John at his home on McChord AFB when the kids were young. I was still trying to get used to their names. Kevin was the second child of three boys and the youngest, a girl. At one point I asked, "You're Kevin?" He said, "No." I had been fairly sure I was right, but maybe not. "Brian?" I said. "No." "Thomas?" "No." This youngster of like 6 or 7 totally messed with me.

166

Brian and Thomas were both there at the memorial when I shared that story for the first time.

I also added a time of mourning for Aunt Annie who took a distant backseat for most there to Kevin's memorial.

Amy and I had ridden with Jay, so headed to town to do our dinner shopping for the big group. We took the time to drive around a bit and reminisce when dad and mum lived there. When we returned, the sun had decided to make an appearance. I just hung-out by the firepit on a folding chair to bask and lightly nap. Perfect!

The Hiss clan came to the service, so I got to visit with Aunt Jeanne whom I'd not seen since 1999 when my dad died. Her son Steven I'd also not seen for many years, yet readily recognized. Her oldest, Jeff, and second child, Charlene, came with their spouses and lived in Washington, so I'd seen both of them many times over the years.

Before dinner, my seven-year-old grandson wanted to play horseshoes with Grandpa. He would be closer to the stake, of course, which meant he totally skunked me. I suggested his moving back from the stake, but he declined because, in his words, he was so good a horseshoe player. Afterward, he made sure everyone there knew he beat Grandpa.

Liam's sister Finley still called Amy "Nanny". We'd wondered if she'd remember. Amy and Finley colored and did crafts a bunch in the RV. Amy also gave Finley rides on her scooter. We probably mildly irritated their mum, Alicia, because we gave them more small toys that she would have preferred not be given. As grandparents, we already don't see them enough.

Pulled pork became the centerpiece for the dinner with lots of yummy additions.

That night, around the campfire with our guitars, I was amazed when my cousin Steven requested *Apple Valley, (By Victorville),* a song I'd written in 1974. Hitchhiking from Redlands, CA to Ogden, I spent the night in Apple Valley – a most memorable night, so wrote a song about it. Aunt Jeanne asked for the story behind the song.

In 1975, after I'd enlisted in the Navy, I was stationed in Groton, CT for submarine training school. Uncle Roger was a Navy officer who served on submarines. I'd followed his lead, enlisting in the Navy and volunteering for submarines. The latter actually had been a big mistake. I was 6'7" at the time, (I've lost a couple inches over the years), and submarines were built for people 6'3" and shorter. I could not stand up straight when I walked through the boat, (submarines are called boats, not ships). My bed was a hole in the wall, also 6'3" long, so I could not stretch out straight. It was obnoxious, but I was young & immortal then, so could traverse around the boat as fast as anyone.

Submariners are also a very strange group. Just before heading out to sea, one of my co-workers showed me his coloring book and crayons. They commonly danced together in the dining room. They played tricks on one another constantly. They could not go up on deck in the nuclear-powered boats. The old diesel boats had to stay on the surface most of the time because they had a tailpipe. A sailor could climb up into the top of the sail anytime, day or night. There was always an officer on duty in the sail, watching the sea and just up there to chat with when you came up. I had spent a month on the USS Salmon, a diesel powered sub, that was decommissioned within two years after my temporary tour of duty. I appreciated being able to spend some off time up in the sail while out to sea.

The nuke subs didn't need to stay on the surface, and my boat, the USS John Marshall, a Polaris Class sub, would go out to sea, submerge and stay submerged the entire three months. It would often "skim" just under the surface, to take in fresh air, for radio communications and even the telescope which it didn't use often. Nope, it wasn't like those old WWII movies you'd seen.

Piloting such a boat is a trip because you cannot see where you're going. There are no windows. Two sailors man the driver's seats, one doing the driving while the other makes sure it doesn't go too deep. I expect a four-hour shift driving such a craft would get very, very boring, yet if I'd had any good sense at the time, I would've been a Quartermaster rather than a Commissaryman, ie, Cook or Steward. I've always loved maps and certainly would have had a much better Navy experience doing something I liked.

So, in 1975, stationed in Groton, the main sub-base on the Northeast Coast, attending Submarine training, I got to visit with my aunt and cousins a whole bunch. I was a young guitar player at the time, just trying his hand at songwriting. I'd not written a dozen songs as yet. *Apple Valley* was one of the more fun songs I'd written. So, for cousin Steven to remember it after all these years was amazing and to be honest; very honoring. Thank you, Steven.

Back in '75, I'd brought to their house a 45 RPM record of the *Archies*. We tried to remember which song it was. Some minutes later, I remembered it was *Bang-Shang-a-Lang*.

After playing Apple Valley, my brother John asked if I would play *Spice and Raisin Songs*. I'd co-wrote that one with another sailor, Don Childress. Actually "stole" is a better word. Don wrote the song which I learned at sub school. I loved it. We parted company in Connecticut, only to get together again in Vallejo, CA and again on Oahu, Hawaii. I never learned Don's words to the song, so composed my own. I've not seen Don since. I even looked him up on Facebook a couple of times. *Spice and Raisin Songs* has been one song I've played regularly when I did gigs.

Just another sidenote, in 1975 I wrote a song for Don, aptly named *Don*. He was engaged at the time and having second thoughts, so *Don* is a song of encouragement – kind of. He wound up not marrying the girl, name Joy. When I saw him again in Hawaii in 1976, he was with another girl. (I did not write another song about them.)

My sister Teresa and Jay had worked on re-wording a song to sing for Kevin. She wanted to sing it at his memorial, but was not ready. Practicing with Jay a few more times that afternoon, she was ready to share. More tears and sweet feelings around the campfire.

The guitars and music continued until after 1 a.m. to end the day. Having a group campground, you don't usually have to worry about making too much noise for the neighboring campers. As long as we weren't shooting off fireworks or firing handguns, nobody outside our camp would notice we were there.

TUESDAY, JULY 27th

Another day at the camp. Amy and I were part of dinner crew that day.

At previous year's reunions, we always got together for more than three days, except in 2000 at the Refugio Beach reunion near Santa Barbara, CA. That was all the days we could reserve.

During the day, Uncle Ray was walking from someone's camp, back to the central grassy area. He stepped off a small ledge and fell on the grass. We saw him go down, ran to help, and checked him before getting him back to his feet. My brother Bob is a Respiratory Therapist in a hospital, so knows at least a bit more than most about medical conditions and what to check for. We determined nothing was broken though he had some pain in one leg. We got one of my walking sticks for him to use which he appreciated, then didn't need after a short time. We were all supremely glad he was okay. At 87, he still does more than most.

For dinners, we'd typically have a new dinner cooked each night except the last night, then all the leftovers would come out, and we'd help gobble down the last of the week's grub. This shorter reunion never saw the leftovers night.

Cooking with brother Jay and my son Paul, we decided on Thai chicken. Amy and I cooked the rice, (not fried rice). Our donation to the dinner was $115, (not just for rice.)

It took much longer than expected to cook that much rice for that many people. Learn as we will, we'll be sure to cook it in separate batches thereafter. Even worse, the rice at the bottom stuck together terribly, surely in part by the weight of the rice on top. I'm in awe since I've seen similarly sized pots filled with rice at Chinese restaurants. Still, there was more than plenty of perfectly cooked rice, and nobody was stuck with the globby mass at the bottom. On the other hand, it was a Thai meal. We could've said it was Sticky Rice.

Paul is a hot sauce affectionado. I ate lots of very hot food when I was young. Not so much nowadays, though I still have a bit of an asbestos tongue. Paul gets sauces that were much hotter than anything out when I was his age.

My tolerance for hot food was an accident. First, our mother did not cook spicy food. When we were teens, all the boys in my neighborhood would get a vial of real cinnamon oil from one of the local pharmacies. There were two small pharmacies near my home in Ogden. We'd cram the small bottle full of toothpicks, set it somewhere out of sight, and forget about it for literally six to twelve months. I declare, it was the only self-disciplined thing I did as a child. After the toothpicks had that long to absorb every molecule of cinnamon oil, they were viciously hot. You touched it to your lips and tongue to suffer greatly, but it was so good.

When I went out on my own in 1973, I stayed with Uncle Ray for a spell. He loved hot food, so one night made a Mexican dish with lots of jalapenos or Anaheim peppers and who knows what other peppers. I knew it would be too hot for me to eat it but buckled down to make the best of it. I ate and chewed and swallowed, and to my surprise, it wasn't that hot at all, yet it made me sweat eating it. My nose also got runny. It was years before I realized my tolerance for hot foods probably

172

came from eating those homemade cinnamon toothpicks all those years.

Well, Paul has exceeded my asbestos mouth by quite a bit. He had one blistering sauce I tried. It was good and it was hot, but not unenjoyable – for a bit. As you continued eating, even if you didn't have anymore of the hot sauce, it got hotter and hotter in your mouth. My brother Bob and I tried putting more of the super-hot sauce on it. I decided it was too hot to enjoy my food, dumped it and got some more food. Bob kept eating, I'm sure not enjoying it a bit. Paul teased him about that as well, but Bob would not be deterred. I doubt he had much stomach lining left the rest of the night, not to mention a throbbing tongue and palette that no amount of foamy beer could douse. Nope. Like the food, the suds made your mouth feel hotter.

To this day, I like hot food, but it still has to be a flavor I like. For example, I like the flavor of jalapenos better than Chinese mustard.

By the third day, everyone has had a chance to chat and get caught up on life. Things begin to lull a little – not a bad thing, especially as all us kids are getting older. Mum's still alive, but I wonder at times if we'll continue the reunions after she's gone? I called her the Matriarch, but to be honest, she's a very humble and loving person who's just nice to visit with. One of these years I'm expecting she'll still be with us but unable to make the reunion. We'll see.

One big highlight for the evening – Bill knew the space station would be passing overhead after 10 p.m. He knew within a minute or two when it should pass overhead, so we left the light of the fire to watch the sky. Someone caught sight of a satellite – a small dot slowly crossing the sky. Nothing all that remarkable, and we thought that might be it. Then, it appeared shortly thereafter, much brighter. Oohs and aahs. Fun to see.

Mum, Bill and Jeanne, and my other sister Teresa left for the hotel thereafter. That would be the end of the reunion for them. Same for Uncle Ray.

We returned to the fire and played more music, including *Dear Prudence*, and some Neil Young songs with Jay playing harmonica. The group broke up after midnight.

WEDNESDAY, JULY 28th
End of the reunion.

We talked about having another reunion in 2022. They'd always been every two years, and thereby during even numbered years, not that that mattered. Some called this not a reunion, but a memorial for Kevin, so suggested we have an official reunion next year. Nothing was finally decided, but I expect we shan't get together next year.

The morning of the last day is typically everyone packing up to go. Hugs and kisses good-bye. That sort of thing. Being in the motorhome, it doesn't take that long to pack-up compared with many of the others. It took longer to secure the bike and scooter than anything else. Thereafter, I got to see to others, see if they needed anything, and so forth.

Bob had been seeing a woman named Cherie who'd come to the previous two reunions in the Grand Tetons and near Newberg, OR where Amy and I got married in 2018. Bob was our photographer and she pitched right in to help. Then, this reunion she didn't come. I'd not heard they were apart or broke-up, so asked. Bob said that they'd parted company, partially over her daughter, Bella.

We said our good-byes to the grandkids, then others, and I thought we'd be out of there before half a dozen other campsites, but as it turned out, we were the last ones leaving. Our campsite took us around the rest of the loop. Yup. Everyone else was already gone. Wow! They'd finished packing up quickly and took off without another word.

This was a funny moment, not because everyone was gone, but because we honestly did not know where we were going. We had considered ending the trip and heading back home after the reunion, but there were two other Washington stops that we could not see earlier – Amy's Aunt Stella and Uncle Larry who lived in Richland, and my Uncle Larry and Aunt Barbara in Wenatchee. We called Larry "Skunkle" Larry.

Back on the road, Amy contacted her Aunt Stella and we were welcome to drop in for the day or two. Same answer from Skunkle Larry, so we headed first for Richland.

We were low on diesel, but for no good reason than to save a few bucks, I avoided filling up on the coast. I headed inland towards Corvallis with less in the tank than I should have. We made it to Philomath where we filled up, and I really believed the entire drive that we would have enough fuel, but I admit I was sweating bullets at times. Thank You, Jesus!

Next, we got to enjoy Portland rush hour traffic. It went fairly well with only a few terrible slowdowns. One time a box semi beside us literally started coming into our lane. I had to slam on brakes to get behind without being hit.

We would cross the Columbia on I-205 for Highway 14 and the eastbound road towards Richland. Before leaving civilization, we stopped for ice and drinks. I tried carrying four bags of ice and drinks out to the RV. Silly me. I dropped one of the ice bags, splitting it open – better than the drinks, I guess.

We didn't try to make it all the way to Richland that day. Both of us had driven through the Gorge many times. One road I'd never taken was Highway 14 following the north side of the Columbia River. I'd wished to take it many times, so today would be the day. We found vacancy at Wind Mountain RV Park near Stevenson, WA. Not the fanciest, and prices a little higher than they should be for what they offered. No laundry or showers. The office closed the whole time we were there.

The RV next to us had an American flag lit up sign in their window that shown into our motorhome all night. We never said anything, as actually the extra light was fine and provided good light when you walked out of the RV. Two friendly, beer drinking dudes playing cornhole across the street from us let us know what was and was not available there.

We'd planned on cooking dinner over our camp stove, then discovered that the little, screw-on propane tanks I'd bought didn't fit. Different fittings on the stove than I'd ever seen, so we had to cook inside – not a big deal, and just another thing we didn't test before we left.

THURSDAY, JULY 29th

Leaving Wind River, we continued along Highway 14. I kept eyes open for a place to stop and look at the river. We passed the entrance to Horse Thief Lake picnic area. It looked wonderful as I continued, better able to see the place after I'd passed the entrance. I figured there would be more places to stop, but I was wrong. That was the best and really the only one.

Later, we stopped at a boat ramp by the Columbia River. Some people were tent camping and it had decent pit rest rooms. We enjoyed the little rest from driving, but it was far from as nice as Horse Thief Lake. The pond that received the boats was not anything anyone would want to even wade through. It had a small, wooden pier. A sizeable dead fish floated right next to the pier.

We also stopped at a high View Point overlooking the Columbia. A couple on a Harley, stopped as well and chatted. They hailed from Edmonds, WA, a city north of Seattle. From Sequim, we sometimes took the Kingston to Edmonds ferry.

We also passed through a small town with a bakery that had the big letters GF on the side. Amy knew it meant Gluten Free, so we turned around and got some goodies through the drive-thru, that she could eat for breakfast.

Approaching Richland, we left Highway 14 for Patterson Rd. – a rather regular two-lane through farm country. There's a small escarpment we swung through, but mostly it was farmland. Eventually, we reached I-84 and landmarks we better recognized.

Stella and Larry previously had a lovely home in a newer neighborhood. Our last visit, touring their yard, Stella said they were going to sell the house. It'd become too much for them to maintain. So, they had a small house built on the back lot of property where their son Brigham and his family had lived, right on one of the small highways into town. Sadly, Brigham and his wife had split up over the previous year, so property and such were still being sorted out. She was still living in the house with the kids, but the property was owned by Stella and Larry, so she would have to vacate sometime soon. The grandkids could stay as long as they wanted. I don't know how it's turned out, if anything, since our visit.

Brigham had a large shop right next to the house. He collected a few antique guitars, so invited me to his shop to see his collection for me to play them upside-down. (I play guitar left-handed). We talked about music a bit – probably the best solo chat I'd ever had with Brigham to date.

Leaving the cool coast, we were hit smack in the face with hundred plus degree weather in Richland. As soon as we arrived, we had to get Morris plugged in and AC running. Brigham's shop would be perfect for that, but they'd installed 15 amp plugs throughout for the 120 Volt, and it kept tripping the breakers. It took a bit of trial and error, but we finally made it work with his 30 amp plug for his welder. The hardest part there was getting a cord long enough to reach the RV.

Visits at Stella and Larry's are always an adventure. This time we had Stella's grandkids, Bella and Joyce, who dropped-in anytime they wanted, walking down from the upper house. Amy played lots of games with them.

Stella and Larry are very liberal – very Democrat. Amy and I are far more conservative – not always Republican, but definitely more conservative, so the conversations always at some point become very emotional, especially between Amy and Stella. At one point after they'd been yelling at one another, I grabbed the lull to say to Larry, "Loveya Larry." It was the perfect reminder of what's important between family members.

Larry and I mostly talked church, sitting outside as the hot temperatures started to decline for the day. Outside we did not have to compete with the TV or Amy and Stella's not-too-heated-but-still-louder debates. Of course, neither of them changed anyone's mind about anything.

With that said, that's just who she is. She's very passionate about what she believes. There's a little of the "I already know what I believe. Don't confuse me with the facts," but that's okay. Her saltiness is just part of her personality. It happens every visit and yet we always look forward to seeing them again.

The Olympics were going on, so we watched lots of track and field events as well as swimming.

As dinner approached, they offered to take us out to Isla Bonita Mexican Restaurant. Nope, we were not tired of Mexican food yet in any way, shape or form. Very yummy. Stella got a plate big enough for her to eat for the next four days.

We gratefully got cleaned up for the evening and had a nice sleep in our little home away from home, away from politics and such.

FRIDAY, JULY 30th

Stella made a wonderful breakfast – much more than everyone could eat. We watched more Olympics, still mostly swimming and running. Then, Amy wanted to see her friend Stephanie who lived a few miles outside Richland. Stella let us take her car. We had a very sweet visit, staying until after 1 a.m. I'd not met her before. Back at Stella's, I snuck in the front door to leave the car keys.

SATURDAY, JULY 31ˢᵗ
Destination: Wenatchee

We departed Richland early to get beyond the worst of the heat. We said our good-byes and hugs shared. I mentioned Stella's love of chaotic arguing, but that's just part of her family's personality. Amy's mom likes to argue with Kyler, her grandson, having some knock down and drag outs, but still love each other deeply. Stella is Jackie's older sister. They like to blame one of the family strains for their confrontative habits.

We were super blessed to be able to add Wenatchee as the last stop of our trip to see Skunkle Larry and Aunt Barbara. It was supposed to be one of the first stops, but they had other family commitments out of town back in June.

Skunkle Larry is one of a kind. Somewhat loud and strongly opinionated, yet jovial and totally likable. Ten years my senior, I was the obnoxious brat he sometimes had to play with outside when the adults were visiting, or had to ride with in the back of the car when going to a California beach. Both conservatives politically today, we have become much closer over the last decade or two, in part thanks to cell phones and the ease of sending each other notable posts and videos.

Aunt Barbara is almost the opposite to her husband. She's sweet as can be, much quieter, yet has certainly learned to hold her own alongside her sometimes obnoxious husband. Both look surprisingly spry for being in their mid-70's.

When I entered their home, the first thing Aunt Barbara said to me was, "We have been exposed to COVID by the grandchildren. Is that a problem?

I certainly did not want to catch any disease, but I figured we had all been exposed to it just shopping at Walmart, masks or no masks. No apprehensions on our part to stay and visit. It turned out to be one of the sweetest stops of our entire adventure.

Their youngest daughter Jennifer and her husband John also live with them in their large home. Jennifer is an elementary school teacher, and John a construction contractor. They'd recently bought a sizable chunk of land, then even more recently leveled it on a mountainside, for John to build their dream home. We'd not met John before this visit.

Amy was sleeping when we arrived, and stayed in bed a little later. Eventually, she appeared to be greeted by leftover soup, crackers and cheese. Then, Larry and I backed Morris up their very long, very uphill driveway. He guided me up. I had to correct a couple times, turning too early or something. Skunkle Larry had a large RV and knew all the pitfalls to avoid along the way. I parked alongside it.

They had placed a swimming pool in their driveway and filled it with water. It wasn't really set-up to be anything besides a place to cool-off during the hot days. It was a hot day though cloud covered. Their oldest child, Matt, and wife Vicki came over to see us. Matt took a cool-off dip in the pool while John and I chatted with him on the driveway concrete.

As dinnertime approached, Larry and Barb wanted to take us out to Buzz On Steakhouse. Pretty good food, though the plastic covered menus were dirty, sticky and definitely not cleaned anytime if at all, all day. Pretty gross.

We had the big, family table for ten of us. Much revelry and fun, sharing food and laughter. Even after we paid and stood outside, we still chatted at length with Matt and Vicki who would be heading for home from there. Then, back at Larry and Barbara's, we sat out on their covered patio all evening.

As I indicated, they live on a hillside with a sweet overlook of the city and Columbia River. Unfortunately, the Oregon forest fires brought much smoke congestion. Anything further than a few miles could not be seen at all. I believe the smoke was worse here than Winnemucca.

After evening showers, Amy and I accepted their hospitality to sleep indoors.

Dave With Uncle Larry and Aunt Barbara

SUNDAY, AUGUST 1st

Being Sunday morning, we had to go to church. Larry and Barbara attended All Apostles Catholic Church in Wenatchee. Very lovely church. One remarkable feature is that the floor with the pews slants down towards the altar. The pews you sit on are slightly tilted forward. Not a big deal, but remarkable.

They had some students from the local Catholic School come speak and invite people to have their children consider coming to the Catholic school.

Amy needed a prescription refill. Fortunately, we were able to get it, similar to our experience in Lincoln, NE. John and I went for haircuts at Great Clips. Lazy afternoon thereafter. Amy napped – one of her favorite activities. Barbara later made chicken for dinner. We ate outside. Still smoky, but a cooler day, so hung-out outside the rest of the evening until dinner.

Jennifer offered to collect some plant starts out of the yard for Amy to replant when we got home.

MONDAY, AUGUST 2nd

Homeward Bound. Very sad but still very good. It had been a great trip – one for the books, pun intended. We departed Larry and Barb's after breakfast. Took pics of all of us by Morris. Jenny had collected the plants for Amy, so we stowed them safely.

There are some sweet, curvy roads leaving Wenatchee. Also, the town of Leavenworth is just a few miles west of Wenatchee. Amy and I had been there before and really enjoyed the German theme, but for today, it was time to go home. She was ready to return to Sequim and a little of our old lives.

Thus, we turned south on Highway 97 through the Wenatchee Mountains. The road leaves 97 for 970 to reach westbound I-90. When you're driving east, the climb up to the top of Snoqualmie Pass is long, but from the east side heading west, not much uphill at all. You're already on the up and up. We cruised down into some Seattle-Tacoma traffic – approaching rush hour. Still not quite bumper to bumper.

We got home around 3 p.m. I looked at the odometer. 7,530 miles from when we left June 18th – 46 days earlier. The doggies greeted us ecstatically. We said hi to the kids, gave them their gifts and settled in for an hour or so to rest. Then, I got the extension cord to Morris, and brought in all the food out of the fridge. A few personal items came in, but not much else. That would wait till tomorrow.

The house was a bit dirty. They kids somehow thought we would be home the next day or something. Or, that's what they said they thought. There were a bunch of dead plants. Quinnlyn had been in charge of

186

watering out back. Didn't happen much if at all. Our little circle of grass in the backyard was also pretty much dead with a few weeds left to thrive. We watered all.

I'd planted potatoes for the first time this year. Since the plants were looking less than healthy from lack of water, I went ahead and harvested all potatoes I could find. Actually, it turned-out to be a nice harvest of red potatoes – enough for three or four meals.

I brought the extension cord out to power Morris.

The black cat was still here. Quinnlyn had named her Bennie.

EPILOG

It's been some months since we got home. It did not take very long before we were thinking the trip felt like a long time past. Amy had to go back to work at the school district. I had other matters that demanded attention and kept me more than busy through August and well into September. I gladly share the bottom line for having the really Grand Adventure we'd been wanting. Before the trip, we'd considered spending the money flying to Europe, but that would have been a much shorter trip. Maybe next year if we have the money.

Our original plan was to sell Morris when we got home. Recoup some of our costs. We still have Morris as of mid-October, 2021. The deciding factor will be if we think we'll travel in him over the next year or two. If not, then we will sell him for sure. As much as we enjoyed having this old but comfortable motor home, it would be a waste to just let him hang out unused in the driveway.

With that said, the way things are going in the US this year, maybe a motorhome would be a good thing to have for when our society comes crashing down to an absolute halt. We could find a private mountain somewhere, or even sneak across the border for a few nights. We'll see. I don't really expect that much of a cataclysm as yet, but one never truly knows.

I'm a travelaholic, a driveaholic and a perpetual wanderlust. Even as I sit here typing, I would prefer to be in my convertible with the top down, driving in warmer climes.

If and when there is a next trip, we might get gas powered scooters so we have transportation that can go many miles around town and down tree lined dirt roads, so does not require we drive the big box to explore the area. Regular bicycles are nice, but a bit sore on the underside bones to ride further than a few miles.

My recommendation – if you seek a blessed way to see the nation and have the money to go, there are plenty of RV's available for sale. A little patience can bring you one that's a better buy for the money. There are plenty of RV life lessons online. I watched plenty of them before we left.

There are always a few things we'd do differently, (beyond not forgetting my sandals again or losing gas caps). Likewise, though Morris performed so amazingly well, we should have been a bit more investigative before making the purchase. Being two hours from home to test drive Morris in Olympia, life not convenient to just drop-in to see Maurice when we had another question. Things like working turn signals and headlights we should have checked before buying. Basic schtuff.

This week, as I finish this book, I entered Morris, parked in our driveway, and sighed. It still feels a bit like home every time I enter. I would have been glad to live in that little box for a few more months and probably negotiate for even more time after that.

* Many Thanks to you for sharing time with me and Amy in our adventures across America.
Your Reviews are greatly appreciated.

Feedback also always welcome.

May God's blessings be ever with you in your walk with Jesus and His Holy Spirit.

If you like the book, please review it.
It's very helpful for letting others know what you thought.

Other Books by David Stoeckl

- Patmos – An Apostle in Exile – A Planet on Trial (a Historic, Biblical novel)
- Patmos also available as an Audiobook
- Life's Vagabondage (an Allegorical novel)
- Life's Vagabondage Audiobook (soon coming)
- Tossing Mountains – Where are the Miracles Today Like We Read About in the Bible?
- Silhouette of God – A Bit of Poetry
- Oops! There Goes Another One (a novel)
- Julesburg Cruisin' Night (a Pictorial)
- An Awful Lot Like Me (a novella)
- Amy and Dave's Glacier Escape Tour - 2025
- Amy and Dave's Portugal Escape Tour – 2023
- Amy and Dave's COVID Escape Tour – 2021
- Your Quick Guide to Understanding Subsidized Housing (How to apply for HUD Housing)
- His Heart Art – a Devotional   (pen name David Sterling
- 52 Diets a Year (pen name David Sterling)
- 40 Days Christian Devotional (Pending)

(& More To Come)